KAKE BRAND Cookbook

JESS MITCHELL

A Martin Book

Martin Books
8 Market Passage, Cambridge CB2 3PF

First published 1980
© C H Dempster & Co. Ltd. and Jess Mitchell 1980
ISBN 0 85941 119 2

Conditions of sale
All rights reserved. No part of this publication may be reproduced, stored in a retrieval system or transmitted, in any form or by any means, electronic, mechanical, photocopying, recording or otherwise, without the prior permission of the copyright owners.

Design by Ken Vail
Typesetting by A-Line Services, Saffron Walden
Printed and bound in Great Britain by Hazell Watson & Viney Limited, Aylesbury, Buckinghamshire

CONTENTS

Foreword 5

Kake Brand and Chocolate 6

Family Favourite Chocolate Cakes 7
Beat the Clock Chocolate Cake 9
Jamaican Swirl Cake 10
Westhaven Cake 12
Cherry Choc-o-nut Loaf Cake 13
Beverley Duncan's Chocolate Cake 14
Valencia Cake 14
Chocolate Fudge Cake 16
Weekend Marble Cake 18
Chocolate Orange Cake 20
Chocolate Swiss Roll 21
Caramel Sandwich Cake 22
Chocolate Banana Buns 24
Orange Chocolate Top-nots 24
Jaffa Cakes 25
Chocolate Mousse Tarts 26
Chocolate Eclairs 28

Chocolate Gâteaux 29
German Chocolate Layer Cake 29
Rhoda's Chocolate Cake 32
Pear and Chocolate Gâteau 33
Austrian Chocolate Cake 34
Victoria's Chocolate Cake 36
Victoria Sponge 37
Chocolate Boxes 37
Alphabet Bricks 38
Colettas 40

Family Puddings and Pies 41
Banana Jewel Pie 41
Pineapple Crunch Pie 42
Fairy Meringue Pie 44
Chocolate Apple Crunch Pie 45
Dreamy Chocolate Pie 46
Chocolate Mousse 47
Chocolate Chip Steamed Pudding 47
Old Farmhouse Chocolate Pudding 48
Hot Chocolate Soufflé 49
Chocolate Rice Pudding 49
Austrian Chocolate Pudding 50

Cold Sweets for Special Occasions 51
Scrumptious Mocha Pie 51
Oregon Chocolate Soufflé 52
Chocolate Dessert Cups 53
Chocolate Chalet Gâteau 53
Chocolate Belgravia 54
Raspberry or Pear Meringue Gâteau 56
Chocolate Pavlova 57
Pots-au-Chocolat 58

Sauces, Spreads, Fillings and Frostings 60
Hot Chocolate Sauce (with variations) 60
Chocolate Sauce 60
Chocolate Orange and Walnut Sauce 61
Chocolate and Spiced Rum Sauce 61
Dreamy Chocolate Cream 62

Rich Chocolate Butter Cream Filling 62
American Chocolate Frosting 64
Chocolate Butter Cream 64
Very Special Chocolate Cream 64

Tray Bakes 65
Fudgy Brownies 65
Toffee Nut Bars 66
Date and Nut Crunchy Bars 66
Coconut Delight 68
Crunchy Crunchies 69
Millionaire's Shortbread 69
Fruity Chocolate Squares 70
Chocolate Mint Fingers 71
Fudgy Chocolate Fingers 72
Viennese Biscuit Cake 72
Simple Florentines 73
Chewy Chocolate Squares 73
Raisin Bars 74

Biscuits 75
Crunchy Cookies 75
Disneyland Cookies 76
Carolina Cookies 76
Danish Cookies 77
Spicy Ice Box Cookies 77
Chocolate Orange Biscuits 78
Chocolate Mallows 80
Viennese Shorties 81

Home-made Sweets 82
Rum Truffles 82
Chocolate Peppermint Creams 84
Chocolate Ginger Creams 84
Raisin Bon-bons 84
Tutti-frutti Chocolates 85
Oriental Macaroons 85
Chocolate Ginger Balls 86
After Dinner Mints 86
Chocolate Liqueurs 88
Chocolate Marzipan Brazils 88

Fun for the Kids 89
Coconut Kisses 89
Snowballs 90
Chocolate Coconut Chews 90
Nutty Crunchies 92
Chocolate Krispies 92
Chocolate Marshmallows 92
Chocolate Dates 93
Chocolate Banana Triangles 93

Definitely Different Chocolate Drinks 94
Royal Hot Chocolate 94
Chocolate Egg Nog 94
Spanish Chocolate 95
Rich Iced Chocolate 95

FOREWORD

by Norman Mude,
Sales Director, Kake Brand

When it was suggested that this company should sponsor this book, I was delighted because I had been collecting recipes for just such a purpose for many years—as long ago, in fact, as 1967 when I was first appointed as Sales Manager for Kake Brand.

It was particularly fitting that Kake Brand should do this because the product now known as "Chocolate Flavoured Cake Covering" was invented by them in 1955. Since then, we have come a long way—most of it in a hurry. However, we have never been too busy to make friends, both in the trade and in the home and, some of the recipes in this book have been sent in to us by housewives who just wanted to let us know how much they enjoyed using our product. To them we are grateful, as we are to all our own team of demonstrators who have contributed ideas and recipes.

Jess Mitchell was the obvious choice to write the book. As well as being a highly skilled home economist, broadcaster and author, she is a close friend and has been in charge of our demonstration service in Scotland for more years than either of us care to acknowledge. Few people know more about working with Kake Brand than she and her down-to-earth and commonsense approach to the subject will, I hope, make this book as much fun for you to use, as it has been for us to evolve.

KAKE BRAND AND CHOCOLATE

The story of chocolate is a fascinating one and starts with Cortez' discovery in 1519 that the Aztec Indians were making a frothy beverage from the cocoa bean. It was over a hundred years, however, before it became available in Britain with the establishment of the famous chocolate houses in London.

The cocoa tree is a tropical evergreen with small pale yellow flowers which issue from "cushions" on the branches and trunk of the tree. They are succeeded by pods about the size and shape of a melon which contain 30–40 beans and these are harvested in May and October. The beans are then fermented and carefully sun-dried before being shipped.

In its natural state, the cocoa bean is almost totally useless because it contains too much cocoa butter for the manufacture of cocoa, and not enough for chocolate. Although a chocolate drink was made in Bristol as early as 1728, it was not until 1828 that Van Houten discovered how to separate the cocoa butter from the cocoa mass. This was the foundation of the multi-million pound chocolate industry as we know it today.

The beans are first roasted, then broken down and ground finely. They are then mixed with sugar, additional cocoa butter is added, and the chocolate is ground again to the right degree of fineness. It is heated and put into a "conche" where in its liquid state it is thoroughly mixed and ground, this process lasting from three to seven days. A very fine texture is thus produced and, at this stage any additional flavouring may be added. Finally it is extruded into moulds and, when set, given its familiar packing.

It is very difficult to use eating chocolate for cooking because, when it is melted, the added fat separates and rises to the surface giving it, when reset, a dull and sometimes streaky appearance. Kake Brand removes this problem entirely by the use of hardened palm kernel oil instead of cocoa butter. This gives it the property of being able to be melted down and reset as often as necessary, always giving a professional gloss.

FAMILY FAVOURITE CHOCOLATE CAKES

Every member of the family loves a chocolate cake, particularly a home-made one, and most Mums have their own favourite recipes which they know will always turn out "right". Like most of you I've created and collected a fair number over the years, so I hope that

these recipes, all well-tried family favourites, will be as successful for you as they have been for me. It's fun to try something new, but remember, careful preparation is important—weigh and measure ingredients accurately and follow the method carefully for guaranteed perfect results every time.

To avoid cracking the covering when cutting Kake Brand coated cakes here are a few tips: Do not coat the cake too thickly. Before cutting, warm the knife slightly so that it slides through the covering. As soon as the Kake Brand is spread, mark with impressions where you wish to cut the cake. Prepare a soft covering by adding margarine or butter in the proportion three parts Kake Brand to one part margarine or butter.

Note: Approximately five sections of Kake Brand are sufficient to cover a 6 in. (15 cm) cake, and four sections equal 1 oz (25 g) approximately.

Luxury margarine refers to table or soft blend margarine, or margarines made with 100 per cent vegetable oil. Creamy white vegetable shortening refers to pure flavourless vegetable fats, such as Trex or Spry. Where sweetened whipped cream is called for, use ½ oz (15 g) sugar to ¼ pint (125 ml) whipped cream.

Quantities of ingredients are given in both imperial (oz, pint) and metric (g, ml) measures; you can use either, *but not a mixture of both*, in any recipe. All spoon measures level unless otherwise stated.

Beat the Clock Chocolate Cake

For the cake
4 oz (125 g) self raising flour
Pinch of salt
1 rounded tablespoon (2×15 ml) cocoa
4 oz (125 g) luxury margarine
5 oz (150 g) caster sugar
2 eggs
1 tablespoon (15 ml) milk
For the filling
2 oz (50 g) Kake Brand (milk or plain), roughly chopped
2 oz (50 g) luxury margarine
1 oz (25 g) caster sugar or soft brown sugar
1 tablespoon (15 ml) boiling water
2 teaspoons (2×5 ml) milk or pouring cream

Sift flour, salt and cocoa into a bowl. Add all other ingredients and beat together until very well blended (2–3 minutes).

Divide mixture evenly between two well greased and bottom lined 7 in. (18 cm) round sandwich tins. Bake in a fairly hot oven, 375°F/190°C/Gas Mark 4, for 25 minutes until well risen and firm to the touch. Cool on a wire tray.

To prepare filling place Kake Brand in a small bowl and melt over hot but not boiling water. Beat together margarine, sugar and melted Kake Brand. Add boiling water and milk and beat again until light and fluffy. When cakes are cold, sandwich together with filling and dredge top with caster or icing sugar.

Jamaican Swirl Cake

For the cake
4 oz (125 g) self raising flour
Pinch of salt
1 rounded tablespoon (2×15 ml) cocoa
2 tablespoons (2×15 ml) boiling water
3 oz (75 g) Kake Brand (milk *or* plain), roughly chopped
3 oz (75 g) margarine
3 oz (75 g) caster sugar
2 tablespoons (2×15 ml) golden syrup
2 eggs
For the filling and topping
2 oz (50 g) Kake Brand (milk *or* plain)
2 tablespoons (2×15 ml) black rum *or* rum essence to taste
8 oz (225 g) icing sugar
2 oz (50 g) luxury margarine

Sift flour and salt. Blend cocoa in boiling water, mix until smooth and allow to cool. Place Kake Brand in a small bowl and allow to melt over hot but not boiling water. Cream margarine, sugar and syrup together until light and fluffy, then beat in the cocoa and melted Kake Brand. Beat in eggs and flour alternately.

Divide mixture evenly between two well greased and bottom lined 7 in. (18 cm) round sponge tins, and bake in a fairly hot oven 375°F/190°C/Gas Mark 5 for 25–30 minutes until well risen and firm to the touch. Cool on a wire tray.

To make the filling and topping, place roughly chopped Kake Brand and rum in a small bowl and melt over hot but not boiling water. Sift icing sugar into a bowl, add margarine and cream together. Add melted Kake Brand and rum. Beat well until light and fluffy.

When cakes are cold, sandwich together with half the filling. Spread remainder on top and using a round bladed knife make a swirling pattern on the surface. Decorate if liked with mimosa balls and angelica leaves.

Melting Kake Brand: place Kake Brand in a bowl over hot but not boiling water and leave to melt.

Westhaven Cake

6 oz (175 g) finely chopped dates
8 fl oz (225 ml) boiling water
1 teaspoon (5 ml) bicarbonate of soda
4 oz (125 g) creamy white vegetable fat shortening
8 oz (225 g) caster sugar
2 beaten eggs
8 oz (225 g) self raising flour
½ teaspoon (2.5 ml) salt
1 tablespoon (15 ml) cocoa
1 teaspoon (5 ml) vanilla essence
6 oz (175 g) Kake Brand (milk or plain), finely chopped or very coarsely grated
2 oz (50 g) chopped walnuts

Pour boiling water over dates, leave to cool and then add bicarbonate of soda. Place creamy shortening cut into small pieces in a large mixing bowl, add caster sugar and beat together until light and fluffy. Gradually beat in the egg. Sift together the flour, salt and cocoa. Add the sifted dry ingredients to the shortening mixture alternately with the date mixture, then add the vanilla essence. Spoon the mixture into a well greased and lined oblong tin 13×9×2 in. (33×23×5 cm) and spread evenly. Mix the Kake Brand and nuts together and sprinkle over.

Bake in a moderately hot oven 350°F/180°C/Gas Mark 4 for 40–45 minutes. Remove from oven and leave in the tin to become quite cold before cutting into squares or fingers.

Cherry Choc-o-nut Loaf Cake

For the cake
6 oz (175 g) self raising flour
1 rounded teaspoon (2×5 ml) baking powder
Pinch of salt
6 oz (175 g) luxury margarine
5 oz (150 g) caster sugar
3 eggs
2 oz (50 g) Kake Brand (milk *or* plain), coarsely grated
1 oz (25 g) chopped walnuts (optional)
For the topping
4 oz (125 g) apricot jam
4 oz (125 g) glacé cherries
2 oz (50 g) walnuts

Sift flour, baking powder and salt into a bowl. Add all the other ingredients and beat together for 2–3 minutes until very well blended.

Spoon mixture into a well greased and lined traditional 2 lb loaf tin or two 1 lb loaf tins, and bake in a moderately hot oven 350°F/180°C/Gas Mark 4 for 50–60 minutes for the 2 lb size and 40–45 minutes for the 1 lb size, until well risen and firm to the touch. To make sure that the cake is cooked through, test with a skewer pushed into centre of cake, and if it comes out clean the cake is ready.

While the cake is cooking prepare the topping. Put jam into a pan and add chopped cherries and chopped walnuts. Stir continuously over a low heat until the mixture comes to the boil. Spread this mixture on top of the cake immediately it comes out of the oven. Leave in the tin to cool.

Beverley Duncan's Chocolate Cake

2 oz (50 g) plain Kake Brand, roughly chopped
4 oz (125 g) luxury margarine
2 oz (50 g) caster sugar
2 eggs
1 tablespoon (15 ml) hot water
4 oz (125 g) self raising flour
½ teaspoon (2.5 ml) baking powder
Pinch of salt

Place roughly chopped Kake Brand in a bowl and melt over hot but not boiling water. Cream margarine and sugar together until light and fluffy. Add eggs one at a time and beat well. Gradually add melted Kake Brand to this mixture, beating well after each addition, then beat in the hot water a teaspoon (5 ml) at a time. Sift together the flour, salt and baking powder and fold into the mixture, using a metal spoon.

Divide the mixture evenly between two well greased and bottom lined 7 in. (18 cm) round sponge tins and bake in a moderately hot oven 350°F/180°C/Gas Mark 4 for 25 minutes until well risen and firm to the touch.

Cool on a wire tray. When cold, sandwich together with whipped cream or Dreamy Chocolate Cream (see page 62) and top with Chocolate Glacé Icing (see page 74) or, if preferred, melted plain Kake Brand.

Valencia Cake

4½ oz (140 g) plain flour
1 teaspoon (5 ml) baking powder
½ teaspoon (2.5 ml) salt
4 oz (125 g) ground almonds
3½ oz (90 g) soft white vegetable fat shortening
6 oz (175 g) caster sugar
3 beaten eggs
3 oz (75 g) Kake Brand (milk or plain), roughly chopped
2 tablespoons (2×15 ml) milk

For a more elaborate decoration for a chocolate cake, coat sides with Chocolate Butter Cream filling, then roll in coarsely grated Kake Brand (milk or plain). This sort of decoration would be suitable for Beverley Duncan's Chocolate Cake.

Sift together flour, baking powder and salt, add ground almonds. Cream shortening and sugar together until very light and fluffy (beat for at least 3 minutes). Gradually beat in the eggs. Then stir in the dry ingredients together with the chopped Kake Brand and the milk. Beat until ingredients are well blended.

Spoon the mixture into a well greased and lined 7 in. (18 cm) deep cake tin and bake in a moderately hot oven 350°F/180°C/Gas Mark 4 for 1¼ hours. To test if cake is cooked, push a skewer into the middle of the cake and if it comes out clean the cake is ready. Cool on a wire tray.

Wrap in foil or cling wrap and store in an airtight tin for two days before cutting.

Chocolate Fudge Cake

For the cake
5 oz (150 g) self raising flour
1 oz (25 g) cocoa
Pinch of salt
6 oz (175 g) butter or luxury margarine
6 oz (175 g) dark soft brown sugar
3 well beaten eggs
2 oz (50 g) plain Kake Brand, roughly chopped
½ teaspoon (2.5 ml) vanilla essence
For the filling and topping
2 oz (50 g) butter or luxury margarine
6 oz (175 g) light soft brown sugar
Finely grated rind and juice of one orange
1 oz (25 g) plain Kake Brand, coarsely grated
6 oz (175 g) icing sugar
For the decoration
2 oz (50 g) plain Kake Brand, coarsely grated

Sift together flour, cocoa and salt. Cream butter or margarine with the sugar until light and fluffy. Gradually beat in eggs adding 1 tablespoon (15 ml) of sifted flour, cocoa and salt with the last addition of egg. Place the Kake Brand in a small basin and stand in hot but not boiling water, and stir until melted. Beat into creamed mixture with vanilla essence. Fold in remaining flour and cocoa. Spoon into a well greased, side and bottom lined, 8 in. (20 cm) deep round cake tin and bake in a moderately hot oven 350°F/180°C/Gas Mark 4 for about 1¼ hours. Turn out and leave to cool on a wire tray.

Put butter, brown sugar, orange juice and rind into a pan and heat slowly, stirring all the time until sugar has dissolved. Remove from heat, add coarsely grated Kake Brand and stir until melted. Stir in sifted icing sugar and beat well until smooth.

Split cake in half and spread over half the filling. Sandwich together and spread the remainder on top, then using a round bladed knife make a swirling pattern on surface.

To decorate put coarsely grated Kake Brand in a strong polythene bag, tie top tightly and place in a bowl of hot water. When Kake Brand has melted remove from water and dry the bag thoroughly. Snip off one bottom corner and trickle Kake Brand in a zig-zag pattern over the top of the cake.

Note: This cake may be baked in two 8 in. (20 cm) round, bottom lined sponge tins in a fairly hot oven 375°F/190°C/Gas Mark 5 for 30–35 minutes. Cool on a wire tray. Fill and decorate as above.

Weekend Marble Cake

6 oz (175 g) plain flour *plus* 1 teaspoon (5 ml) baking powder *or* 6 oz (175 g) self raising flour
2 oz (50 g) cornflour
1 teaspoon (5 ml) baking powder
Pinch of salt
3 oz (75 g) margarine
4 oz (125 g) soft dark brown sugar
1 egg
¼ pint (150 ml) milk
½ teaspoon (2.5 ml) vanilla essence
4 oz (125 g) Kake Brand (milk or plain), coarsely grated

Sift flour, cornflour, baking powder and salt into a bowl. Add margarine cut into small pieces, and rub in until mixture resembles fine breadcrumbs. Add sugar and mix well. Make a hollow in centre of mixture and pour in egg, milk and vanilla essence. Beat with a wooden spoon until thoroughly mixed. The mixture will be rather slack and should just drop off the spoon without the spoon being shaken.

Spoon one third of the mixture into a well greased, side and bottom lined 7 in. (18 cm) round deep cake tin. Sprinkle one third of the grated Kake Brand over the mixture in the tin. Continue adding alternate thirds of cake mixture and Kake Brand, ending with a layer of Kake Brand.

Bake in a moderately hot oven 350°F/180°C/Gas Mark 4 for 1¼ hours. Remove from oven and allow to become almost cold before removing the cake from the tin. This allows the topping to harden.

Chocolate Fudge Cake, Cherry Choc-o-nut Loaf Cake.

Chocolate Orange Cake

For the cake
4 oz (125 g) margarine
4 oz (125 g) caster sugar
Finely grated rind and juice of one orange
6 oz (175 g) self raising flour
Pinch of salt
2 well beaten eggs
4 oz (125 g) Kake Brand (milk or plain), roughly chopped
For the filling
Chocolate Butter Cream (see page 64)
For the topping
½ oz (12 g) butter or luxury margarine
2 oz (50 g) plain Kake Brand
1 teaspoon (5 ml) very strong black coffee
A few drops of vanilla essence

Cream margarine, sugar and orange rind together until light and fluffy. Sift flour and salt. Add beaten eggs and flour alternately to the creamed mixture, finally folding in the chopped Kake Brand and the orange juice.

Divide the mixture evenly between two 7 in. (18 cm) round sponge tins which have been well greased and bottom-lined with greaseproof paper. Bake in a fairly hot oven 375°F/190°C/Gas Mark 5 for 25–30 minutes. Turn out and cool on a wire tray. Sandwich together with Chocolate Butter Cream.

To prepare topping, place all ingredients in a bowl and melt over hot but not boiling water. Pour over the cake and decorate if liked with chocolate cut-outs, or sugared orange or lemon slices.

If preferred this cake may be served with no filling or topping, as two good sized family sponges.

Chocolate Swiss Roll

For the swiss roll
3 eggs
3 oz (75 g) caster sugar
Pinch of salt
A few drops vanilla essence
2 oz (50 g) Kake Brand (milk or plain), roughly chopped
1 tablespoon (15 ml) water
3 oz (75 g) self raising flour
For the filling
¼ pint (150 ml) whipped cream or Dreamy Chocolate Cream (see page 62)

Break eggs into a bowl and add caster sugar, salt and vanilla essence. Whisk until the mixture is really thick and creamy. When thick enough the beater or whisk when lifted from the mixture should leave a trail.

Place the Kake Brand and water in a bowl, stand in hot but not boiling water and stir until the Kake Brand has melted. With a metal spoon fold Kake Brand into eggs and sugar. Sift the flour and carefully fold into mixture using once again a metal spoon.

Pour the mixture into a swiss roll tin 14×10 in. (36×25 cm) greased and lined with greaseproof paper. Level off the surface by tilting the tin. Bake in a fairly hot oven 400°F/200°C/Gas Mark 6 for 10–12 minutes.

Remove from oven and turn out immediately on to a large piece of greaseproof paper. Carefully peel off the lining paper and with a very sharp knife trim off the hard edges. Make a slit along one short side about ½ in. (1.5 cm) from the edge and carefully roll up the swiss roll *with the paper in the inside*. Leave to cool on a cooling tray.

When cold carefully unroll and spread with either whipped cream or Dreamy Chocolate Cream, and re-roll. Dredge top with icing or caster sugar.

Caramel Sandwich Cake

For the cake
4 oz (125 g) margarine
4 oz (125 g) caster sugar
1 packet caramel blancmange powder made up to 4 oz (125 g) with self raising flour
Pinch of salt
1 teaspoon (5 ml) baking powder
2 well beaten eggs
For the filling
Chocolate Butter Cream (*see* page 64)
For the topping
2 oz (50 g) Kake Brand (milk or plain), roughly chopped

Cream margarine and sugar until light and fluffy. Sift together the blancmange powder, salt, flour and baking powder. Add beaten egg and flour mixture alternately to the creamed mixture, beating well after each addition. Divide the mixture evenly between two well greased 7 in. (18 cm) round sponge tins.

Bake in a fairly hot oven 375°F/190°C/Gas Mark 5 for 20–25 minutes. Turn out and cool on a wire tray. When cold, sandwich together with Chocolate Butter Cream.

For the topping place the roughly chopped Kake Brand in a bowl and allow to melt over hot but not boiling water. Pour over top of cake, spread evenly and decorate with chocolate shapes and walnuts.

Caramel Sandwich Cake, Chocolate Orange Cake.

Chocolate Banana Buns

8 oz (225 g) self raising flour
Pinch of salt
1 teaspoon (5 ml) baking powder
2 oz (50 g) margarine
5 oz (150 g) caster sugar
2 well beaten eggs
2 very ripe bananas (mashed)
3 oz (75 g) Kake Brand (milk or plain), coarsely grated

Sift together flour, baking powder and salt. Cream margarine and sugar until light and fluffy, and gradually beat in the eggs alternately with half the flour. Mix mashed banana with the grated Kake Brand and add alternately with the remainder of the flour. Beat well.

Spoon mixture into 24 well greased patty tins or 24 paper cases. Bake in a fairly hot oven 375°F/190°C/Gas Mark 5 for 20 minutes or until well risen and golden brown.

Orange Chocolate Top-nots

2 oz (50 g) margarine
3 oz (75 g) caster sugar
Rind of one orange, finely grated
4 oz (125 g) self raising flour
Pinch of salt
1 beaten egg
2 tablespoons (2×15 ml) orange juice
4 oz (125 g) Kake Brand (milk or plain), coarsely grated

Cream margarine, sugar and orange rind until light and fluffy. Sift flour and salt. Add beaten egg and flour alternately to the creamed mixture, beating well after each addition. Finally beat in orange juice.

Spoon mixture into 12 well greased patty tins or paper cases. Sprinkle grated Kake Brand on top of mixture and bake in a fairly hot oven 400°F/200°C/Gas Mark 6 for 15–20 minutes.

Jaffa Cakes

For the cakes
2 eggs
2 oz (50 g) caster sugar
Pinch of salt
2½ oz (65 g) self raising flour
4 tablespoons (4×15 ml) apricot jam
Finely grated rind of one orange
For the topping
4 oz (125 g) Kake Brand (milk or plain), roughly chopped
2 teaspoons (2×5 ml) cooking oil
1 tablespoon (15 ml) water

Break eggs into bowl, add caster sugar and salt. Whisk until mixture is really thick and creamy. When thick enough the beaters or whisk when lifted from the mixture should leave a trail. With a metal spoon carefully fold in the sifted flour.

Spoon mixture into 18 well greased patty tins and bake in a fairly hot oven 400°F/200°C/Gas Mark 6 for 10 minutes until golden brown and firm to the touch. Remove from tins and allow to cool on a wire tray.

Place jam and orange rind in a pan and warm over a gentle heat. Top each cake with a small teaspoonful of the warm jam and allow to cool.

Put Kake Brand into a small bowl, add oil and water. Place in a pan of hot but not boiling water and allow to melt, stirring well to mix. Leave to cool for 5 minutes and then spoon over the jam. Leave to set.

Chocolate Mousse Tarts

For the pastry
8 oz (225 g) plain flour
Pinch of salt
5 oz (150 g) margarine
2 tablespoons (2×15 ml) caster sugar
2 dessertspoons (2×10 ml) cold water
For the filling
3 oz (75 g) Kake Brand (milk or plain)
1 egg
1 teaspoon (5 ml) top of the milk

Sift flour and salt into a bowl and add the margarine cut into small pieces. Rub margarine into flour until mixture resembles fine breadcrumbs. Make a well in the centre and add the sugar which has been dissolved in the water. Mix well together until pastry resembles a shortbread mixture. Turn on to a floured board and roll out to about 1/8 in. (½ cm) in thickness. Cut into circles and line patty tins. Prick well and bake in a moderate oven 350°F/180°C/Gas Mark 4 for 12–15 minutes. Allow to cool.

Place the Kake Brand in a bowl over hot but not boiling water and allow to melt. Separate the white of egg from the yolk. Beat the white until stiff. Beat the yolk with the top of the milk and add to the melted Kake Brand. Finally fold the egg white into this mixture.

Fill the tart cases and allow to set. Decorate with whipped cream and chopped nuts.

Note: This filling is also suitable to serve as a "quick to make" cold sweet.

Westhaven Cake (cut into squares), Chocolate Banana Buns, Orange Chocolate Top-nots.

Chocolate Eclairs

For the choux pastry
¼ pint (150 ml) water
2 oz (50 g) butter or luxury margarine
2½ oz (65 g) plain flour
2 eggs
For the filling
¼ pint (150 ml) sweetened whipped cream
For the topping
4 oz (125 g) Kake Brand (milk or plain), roughly chopped

Pour water into a pan and add butter or margarine, allow to melt slowly and then bring to the boil. Immediately remove the pan from the heat and add sifted flour all at once. Beat this mixture until it is smooth and leaves the side of the pan. Whisk the eggs slightly and add them gradually to the mixture in the pan, beating all the time. Continue beating until the mixture is smooth and glossy in appearance.

Spoon the mixture into a large piping bag fitted with a plain ½–¾ in. nozzle. Pipe the mixture in lengths 2½–3 in. (6–8 cm) on to lightly greased baking trays, keeping well apart. Bake in a fairly hot oven 400°F/200°C/Gas Mark 6 for 30–35 minutes until the pastry is quite firm and crisp to the touch and pale golden brown in colour. Cool on a wire tray making a small slit in the side of each éclair to let the steam escape.

When cold fill éclairs with whipped cream, then coat each one with melted Kake Brand. As choux pastry tends to soften when filled, I would suggest that the filling and coating with chocolate should be done just about two hours before eating.

CHOCOLATE GÂTEAUX

In this section you will find a selection of really luxurious chocolate gâteaux. Each one is special and has been made by me many times. Don't be doubtful as to your chances of success with some of the unusual ingredient combinations. Just follow the instructions carefully and you, too, can introduce your family and friends to real mouth-watering chocolate specialities.

German Chocolate Layer Cake

For the cake
4 oz (125 g) Kake Brand (milk or plain), roughly chopped
¼ pint (150 ml) cold water
6 oz (175 g) creamy white vegetable fat shortening
12 oz (350 g) caster sugar
4 egg yolks, unbeaten
1 teaspoon (5 ml) vanilla essence
12 oz (350 g) plain flour
1 rounded teaspoon (2×5 ml) bicarbonate of soda
½ teaspoon (2.5 ml) salt
8 fl oz (225 ml) butter milk
6 oz (175 g) desiccated coconut
4 egg whites, stiffly beaten
For the filling
Rich Chocolate Butter Cream (see page 62)
2 oz (50 g) desiccated coconut
2 oz (50 g) finely chopped walnuts or pecan nuts
For the frosting
2 egg whites
12 oz (350 g) granulated sugar
Pinch of salt
3 tablespoons (3×15 ml) cold water
½ teaspoon (2.5 ml) cream of tartar
1 teaspoon (5 ml) vanilla essence
Kake Brand (milk or plain), coarsely grated

Put Kake Brand and water into a small bowl and melt over hot but not boiling water. Allow to cool. Cream shortening and sugar together until light and fluffy. Add egg yolks one at a time, beating well after each addition. Slowly beat in melted Kake Brand and vanilla. Sift flour, bicarbonate of soda and salt together. Add alternately with the butter milk to the egg mixture, beating well after each addition. Mix in the coconut. Carefully fold in the stiffly beaten egg whites.

Divide mixture evenly betweeen three well greased and bottom lined 8 in. (20 cm) round sponge tins. Bake in a moderately hot oven 350°F/180°C/Gas Mark 4 for 40–45 minutes till well risen and firm to the touch. Allow to become quite cold.

With a sharp knife split each cake in half and spread with a layer of Rich Chocolate Butter Cream, to which has been added the coconut and the chopped nuts. Sandwich together and place on a large cake plate or tray.

Put egg whites, sugar, salt, water and cream of tartar into a fairly deep bowl. Place over a pan of boiling water and with a rotary or electric beater beat for about 7 minutes or until frosting thickens and holds its shape in peaks. Remove bowl from boiling water, add the vanilla essence and continue beating until stiff enough to spread over the top and sides of cake. Decorate with coarsely grated Kake Brand.

This is a real party gâteau, sufficient for 18 good wedges. Half quantity of the mixture will make two 7 in. (18 cm) round sponges sufficient for 8 good wedges.

German Chocolate Layer Cake, Rhoda's Chocolate Cake, Pear and Chocolate Gâteau.

Rhoda's Chocolate Cake

For the cake
8 fl oz (225 ml) soured cream
1 teaspoon (5 ml) bicarbonate of soda
6 oz (175 g) caster sugar
2 oz (50 g) Kake Brand (milk or plain), roughly chopped
6 oz (175 g) plain flour
Pinch of salt
1 egg
1 teaspoon (5 ml) vanilla essence
For the frosting
4 oz (125 g) Kake Brand (milk or plain), roughly chopped
4½ oz (135 g) butter or luxury margarine
8 oz (225 g) icing sugar
1 egg, well beaten
1 teaspoon (5 ml) vanilla essence
1 tablespoon (15 ml) lemon juice
4 oz (125 g) chopped walnuts or hazelnuts

Whisk soured cream, bicarbonate of soda and sugar together until very thick. Melt the Kake Brand over hot but not boiling water, and add to the mixture alternately with the sifted flour and salt. Add the egg and the vanilla essence and beat well. Pour the mixture into a well greased side and bottom lined fairly deep 8 in. (20 cm) round sponge tin. Bake in a moderately hot oven 350°F/180°C/Gas Mark 4 for 45 minutes. To test if the cake is cooked push a skewer into the middle of the cake and if it comes out clean the cake is ready. Cool on a wire tray.

Melt the Kake Brand in a good sized bowl over hot but not boiling water. Remove from the heat. Beat in butter or margarine and half sifted icing sugar. Add egg, vanilla essence and lemon juice. Beat well. Add the remainder of the icing sugar and beat well. Finally fold in the chopped nuts.

With a sharp knife cut the cake in half and spread with half the frosting. Sandwich together and spread the remainder on top using a round bladed knife or spatula. Rough the surface so that the frosting stands in peaks.

Pear and Chocolate Gâteau

For the gâteau
4 oz (125 g) Kake Brand (milk *or* plain), roughly chopped
2 tablespoons (2×15 ml) cold water
3 eggs
4 oz (125 g) caster sugar
2½ oz (65 g) self raising flour
Pinch of salt
For the filling and decoration
¼ pint (150 ml) double *or* whipping cream
1 15 oz (425 g) tin pear halves
Very Special Chocolate Cream (*see* page 64)
1 rounded teaspoon (2×5 ml) arrowroot *or* cornflour

Put Kake Brand and cold water into a bowl and melt over hot but not boiling water. Whisk eggs and sugar together until very thick and creamy, or until mixture is thick enough to leave a good trail. Slowly fold in the melted Kake Brand. Sift flour and salt, and carefully fold into mixture using a metal spoon.

Pour mixture into a well greased and lined swiss roll tin approximately 12×8×2 in. (30×20×5 cm) and level off surface by tilting the tin. Bake in a fairly hot oven 375°F/190°C/Gas Mark 5 for 20 minutes until well risen and firm to the touch. Turn out on to a cooling tray, remove paper and allow to cool.

Divide sponge into three equal portions and sandwich together with whipped cream. Place on a suitable sized sandwich tray. Drain syrup from pears and cut each half into four segments. Lay neatly on top of cake. Fill a piping bag with Very Special Chocolate Cream and pipe stars round the top and bottom of cake using a star nozzle.

Blend arrowroot or cornflour with 1 tablespoon (15 ml) of pear syrup. Measure ¼ pint (150 ml) of pear syrup into a saucepan and bring almost to boiling point. Pour over the blended arrowroot. Stir well and return to pan. Cook and stir until mixture thickens and clears. Allow to cool slightly then pour over pears. If liked the glaze may be coloured to a blush pink or pale green.

Austrian Chocolate Cake

For the cake
4 large eggs, separated
3 oz (75 g) caster sugar
4 oz (125 g) Kake Brand (milk or plain), roughly chopped
1½ oz (40 g) self raising flour
Pinch of salt
1½ oz (40 g) fine fresh white breadcrumbs
For the filling and icing
4 oz (125 g) butter or luxury margarine
12 oz (350 g) icing sugar
2 tablespoons (2×15 ml) very strong black coffee
4 oz (125 g) Kake Brand (milk or plain), roughly chopped
1 tablespoon (15 ml) water
2 teaspoons (2×5 ml) cooking oil

Whisk egg yolks and sugar until thick and very pale in colour. Melt Kake Brand over hot but not boiling water. Sift flour and salt and mix with the breadcrumbs. Add alternately to the egg and sugar mixture with the melted Kake Brand, beating well after each addition. Carefully fold in the stiffly beaten egg whites.

Pour mixture into a round fairly deep 8 in. (20 cm) sponge tin, side and bottom lined with greaseproof paper. Bake in a moderately hot oven 350°F/180°C/Gas Mark 4 for 55 minutes. To test if cake is cooked, push a skewer into the middle of the cake and if it comes out clean the cake is ready. Leave cake in tin for 10 minutes, then turn out on to a wire tray to cool.

Cream butter or margarine until soft and add the sifted icing sugar. Beat well until very creamy. Divide the mixture in half. To one half add the coffee and beat well. Melt the Kake Brand, water and oil over hot but not boiling water, and add to the other half. Beat well.

With a sharp knife cut the cake in half and sandwich together with a little of the coffee icing. Spread the remainder over the top and sides of cake, and smooth surface with a hot palette knife. Put chocolate icing into a piping bag with a medium sized star nozzle, piping an attractive design on top. A few pieces of glacé cherry may be added to enhance the decoration.

To make chocolate leaves, choose pliable leaves such as rose leaves, ivy leaves or hibiscus leaves. Wash thoroughly and dry carefully. Coat one side of the leaf with melted Kake Brand. Place on a piece of waxed paper or a wooden chopping board. When dry, carefully peel away the leaf.

Victoria's Chocolate Cake

For the cake
4 oz (125 g) plain Kake Brand, roughly chopped
1 tablespoon (15 ml) milk
2 oz (50 g) ground almonds
4 oz (125 g) caster sugar
3 eggs, separated
For the icing
2 tablespoons (2×15 ml) cocoa
2 tablespoons (2×15 ml) milk
4 oz (125 g) plain Kake Brand, roughly chopped
1 oz (25 g) butter

Put Kake Brand and milk into a bowl and allow to melt over hot but not boiling water. Put ground almonds and sugar into a bowl and mix well. Add the Kake Brand mixture. Add egg yolks one at a time beating well after each addition. Carefully fold in the stiffly beaten egg whites.

Spoon mixture into a well greased, bottom lined 7 in. (18 cm) cake tin and bake in a fairly hot oven 400°F/200°C/Gas Mark 6 for 35 minutes. Turn out very carefully on to a cooling tray. Remove lining paper.

While cake is cooking prepare the icing. Blend cocoa with the milk until smooth, add the Kake Brand and the butter and allow to melt over hot but not boiling water.

Before the cake cools place a plate under the cooling tray. Pour the icing thickly over the cake. The icing which has run down the sides should then be scooped up and poured over again. Repeat for a third time if necessary. Refrigerate overnight.

Provided you follow the instructions carefully, ice when hot and then refrigerate, this should be the most delicious chocolate cake you have ever eaten. Serve small wedges at teatime or with thick cream as a cold sweet.

Victoria Sponge

As the following two recipes require cubes of Victoria Sponge Cake I felt that this would be an ideal spot to give you my own favourite "fail-me-never" recipe. I've used this recipe for more years than sometimes I care to remember. The ingredient combination is very different from the basic Victoria Sponge recipe, so please don't think that the printers have made mistakes.

4 oz (125 g) margarine
6½ oz (190 g) caster sugar
8 oz (225 g) self raising flour
Pinch of salt
3 eggs
7 dessertspoons (7×10 ml) milk
½ teaspoon (2.5 ml) vanilla essence

Cream margarine and sugar until light and fluffy. Add unbeaten eggs, one at a time, beating well after each addition. Add milk and vanilla essence. Sift flour and salt and fold into mixture, using a metal spoon.

Spoon mixture into two well greased 7 in. (18 cm) sponge tins or a well greased oblong tin aproximately 12×8×2 in. (30×20×5 cm), and bake in a fairly hot oven 400°F/200°C/Gas Mark 6 for 25 minutes. Cool on a wire tray.

Chocolate Boxes

8 oz (225 g) Kake Brand (milk or plain), roughly chopped
9 cubes 2×2×2 in. (5×5×5 cm) Victoria Sponge
¼ pint (150 ml) sweetened whipped cream
Apricot or pineapple or tangerine jam
Cherries or chopped nuts and grated Kake Brand for decoration

First prepare some 2 in. (5 cm) chocolate squares by melting the Kake Brand over hot but not boiling water. Spread evenly on to a piece of waxed paper, and as it begins to set mark into squares. When hard, remove from paper. Warm the jam in a small bowl over hot water and coat the sides of the sponge cubes, then press chocolate squares into position to form a box. Pipe a fairly large rosette of whipped cream into the centre of each box and decorate with a piece of glacé cherry, chopped nuts or grated Kake Brand.

Alphabet Bricks

8 oz (225 g) Kake Brand (milk or plain), roughly chopped
9 cubes 2×2×2 in. (5×5×5 cm) Victoria Sponge
2 oz (50 g) butter or luxury margarine
4 oz (125 g) icing sugar
½ teaspoon (2.5 ml) vanilla essence

Melt the Kake Brand over hot but not boiling water. Place sponge cubes on a wire cooling tray and sit the tray on top of a swiss roll tin. Coat each cube with Kake Brand and allow to harden.

Sift icing sugar into a bowl, add butter and cream together until light and fluffy. Beat in vanilla. Using a small star pipe outline the edges of the cubes and with a fine plain pipe write the initials on sides and tops.

To make chocolate cut-outs, spread melted Kake Brand on to waxed paper and leave to set. Using warmed cocktail cutters, cut out shapes. The remaining Kake Brand may be melted and used again.

Colettas

6–8 oz (175–225 g) Kake Brand (milk or plain), roughly chopped
3 oz (75 g) cake crumbs
2 tablespoons (2×15 ml) sherry
1 small tin fruit cocktail
¼ pint (150 ml) sweetened double or whipping cream
3 glacé cherries
Angelica

Put Kake Brand into a bowl and allow to melt over hot but not boiling water. Coat 12 paper cases (use two cases for each Coletta for double strength) with melted Kake Brand, using a fine pastry brush. Leave to harden then coat again and leave to harden.

Soak cake crumbs with the sherry and spoon mixture into chocolate cases, level off with the back of a teaspoon. Spoon fruit cocktail on top.

Peel off paper cases and put into fresh ones. Pipe with large rosettes of whipped cream. Decorate each with a quarter of a cherry and angelica leaves.

FAMILY PUDDINGS AND PIES

The excuse these days for not baking puddings and pies is that we're all counting the calories or Mum is watching Dad's waistline, but I do suspect that most of us really yearn for something sweet to round off a meal. So spoil your family and yourself by trying some of these puddings and pies. There's nothing too difficult or too expensive in the recipes, so, have a go, and give your family a real chocolate treat.

Banana Jewel Pie

For the pie base
3 oz (75 g) Kake Brand (milk or plain), roughly chopped
1½ oz (40 g) margarine
1 tablespoon (15 ml) golden syrup
4 oz (125 g) finely crushed biscuit crumbs
1 oz (25 g) desiccated coconut
For the filling
½ pint (300 ml) red table jelly
3 bananas
Juice of ½ a lemon
¼ pint (150 ml) whipped cream

Melt Kake Brand over hot but not boiling water. Cream margarine and syrup until light and fluffy, then gradually beat in Kake Brand. Mix in biscuit crumbs and coconut. Spoon mixture into an 8 in. (20 cm) flan ring or 8 in. (20 cm) pie plate and press evenly to cover bottom and sides. Allow to set for about 30 minutes.

Make up the jelly. Slice the bananas thickly and toss in the lemon juice. When jelly is almost set add the bananas and pour into the pie case. Allow to set, then decorate with whipped cream.

Pineapple Crunch Pie

For the pie base
3 oz (75 g) Kake Brand (milk or plain), roughly chopped
1½ oz (40 g) margarine
1 tablespoon (15 ml) golden syrup
5 oz (150 g) finely crushed biscuit crumbs
For the filling
1 8 oz (225 g) tin pineapple rings in syrup
1 egg
1 oz (25 g) caster sugar
¼ pint (150 ml) evaporated milk or single cream
Pineapple syrup from tin made up to ½ pint (300 ml) with water
1 oz (25 g) custard powder
Cherries and angelica for decoration

Melt Kake Brand over hot but not boiling water. Cream margarine and syrup until light and fluffy, then gradually beat in Kake Brand. Mix in biscuit crumbs. Spoon mixture into an 8 in. (20 cm) flan ring or 8 in. (20 cm) pie plate. Press evenly to cover bottom and sides. Allow to set for about 30 minutes.

Mix custard powder and sugar to a smooth paste with a little of the fruit syrup. Put remainder of fruit syrup into a saucepan to heat, then pour over custard powder and stir well. Return to pan and bring to the boil stirring constantly. Remove from the heat, stir in beaten egg yolk then gradually beat in the milk. Lay aside one pineapple ring for decoration, chop up remainder and stir into the custard. Leave to cool. Whisk egg white until stiff then carefully fold into the custard. Spoon into pie base. Decorate with pieces of pineapple and angelica. Chill well before serving.

An ice cube tray approximately 10×4 in. (25.5×10 cm) may be used to form the base for this pie.

Chocolate Apple Crunch Pie, Fairy Meringue Pie, Pineapple Crunch Pie.

Fairy Meringue Pie

For the pastry base
8 oz (225 g) plain flour
Pinch of salt
5 oz (150 g) margarine
2 tablespoons (2×15 ml) caster sugar
2 dessertspoons (2×10 ml) cold water
For the spotted meringues
1 egg white
2 oz (50 g) caster sugar
1 oz (25 g) Kake Brand (milk or plain), coarsely grated
For the filling
1 tablespoon (15 ml) custard powder
2 oz (50 g) caster sugar
½ pint (300 ml) milk
3 oz (75 g) Kake Brand (milk or plain), roughly chopped
Few drops of vanilla essence
½ teaspoon (2.5 ml) rum essence (optional)
1 egg yolk
½ oz (15 g) gelatine
2 tablespoons (2×15 ml) cold water
¼ pint (150 ml) chilled evaporated milk

Sift flour and salt into a bowl, add margarine cut into small pieces, and rub into flour until mixture resembles fine breadcrumbs. Make a hollow in the centre and add the sugar which has been dissolved in the cold water. Mix well together with a round bladed knife until it forms a dough in the bowl leaving the sides clean. Turn out on to a floured board or work surface, knead well. Roll out to about ¼ in. (7 mm) in thickness and line an 8 in. (20 cm) fluted flan ring or 8 in. (20 cm) pie plate. Prick well and bake blind in a moderately hot oven 350°F/180°C/Gas Mark 4 for 20–25 minutes until golden brown. Allow to cool.

To prepare spotted meringues, whisk egg white until very stiff, then whisk in half the sugar. Fold in the remainder of the sugar and the coarsely grated Kake Brand. Spoon into a piping bag fitted with a No. 8 star nozzle and pipe small rosettes on to a well greased baking tray. Bake in a cool oven 250°F/130°C/Gas Mark ½ for 50–60 minutes until firm.

Mix the custard powder and sugar to a smooth paste with a little of the milk. Add the Kake Brand to the remainder of the milk and heat slowly. When the Kake Brand has melted bring to the boil. Pour over the custard powder and stir well. Return to the pan and bring to the boil and cook for 2 minutes, stirring constantly. Allow the custard to cool, but stir occasionally to prevent a skin forming.

When cool, add flavourings and mix in the beaten egg yolk. Add gelatine to the cold water and stir until dissolved over hot water. Whisk the chilled evaporated milk until stiff, fold in dissolved gelatine and finally the chocolate custard. Pour into the pastry case. Leave to set. Decorate with meringues, and if liked, whipped cream.

Chocolate Apple Crunch Pie

For the pie base
1½ oz (40 g) margarine
¾ oz (20 g) caster sugar
2 oz (50 g) Kake Brand (milk or plain), roughly chopped
3 oz (75 g) coarse biscuit crumbs
For the filling
2 large cooking apples
2 tablespoons (2×15 ml) caster sugar
Green colouring
1 small tin of full cream evaporated milk, chilled (6 fl oz/ 175 ml) or 5 fl oz (150 ml) whipped cream
1 teaspoon (5 ml) gelatine
1 tablespoon (15 ml) cold water
2 oz (50 ml) Kake Brand (milk or plain), coarsely grated

Melt margarine and sugar in a saucepan over a gentle heat. Melt Kake Brand over hot but not boiling water. Add biscuit crumbs to melted margarine and sugar. Mix well, then stir in Kake Brand. Spoon mixture into a 7 in. (18 cm) flan ring or pie plate. Press evenly to cover bottom and sides. Allow to set for about 30 minutes.

To prepare the filling, peel, core and slice the apples. Stew with a very little water, add sugar and beat if necessary to a purée. Add a few drops of green colouring to give a pleasing apple green colour. Whisk evaporated milk or cream until thick. Add gelatine to the cold water and stir until dissolved over hot water. Stir gelatine into apple purée and fold in cream. Pour into chocolate base, sprinkle with grated Kake Brand and allow to set. Decorate with whipped cream, if liked, and serve well chilled.

Note: Pears may be used in place of apple.

Dreamy Chocolate Pie

For the pie base
1½ oz (40 g) margarine
¾ oz (20 g) caster sugar
3 oz (75 g) coarse biscuit crumbs
For the filling
1 teaspoon (5 ml) gelatine
1 tablespoon (15 ml) cold water
2 oz (50 g) Kake Brand (milk or plain), roughly chopped
1 egg
1 oz (25 g) caster sugar
2 large scoops ice cream (vanilla or coffee)
4 squares Kake Brand (milk or plain), coarsely grated

Melt margarine and sugar in a saucepan over a gentle heat. Add biscuit crumbs and mix well. Spoon mixture into a 7 in. (18 cm) flan ring or pie plate. Press evenly to cover bottom and sides. Allow to set for about 30 minutes.

Add gelatine to the cold water and stir until dissolved over hot water. Melt 2 oz (50 g) Kake Brand over hot but not boiling water. Beat egg and sugar until thick, then fold in the Kake Brand, gelatine and ice cream. Pour into prepared base, sprinkle with grated Kake Brand and allow to set. Decorate with whipped cream, if liked, and serve well chilled.

Chocolate Mousse

6 oz (175 g) Kake Brand (milk or plain), roughly chopped
Knob of butter
1 tablespoon (15 ml) cold water
4 eggs, separated
2 tablespoons (2×15 ml) caster sugar
½ oz (15 g) gelatine plus 1 tablespoon (15 ml) cold water

Put Kake Brand, butter and one tablespoon (15 ml) of water into a large bowl. Melt over hot but not boiling water. Whisk egg yolks and sugar in a bowl over hot water until light and creamy. Add to the Kake Brand mixture. Allow to become cool. Add gelatine to one tablespoon (15 ml) of cold water and stir until dissolved over hot water. Whisk egg whites until stiff and fold into mixture. Add the gelatine and mix well. Pour into individual dishes and allow to set. Decorate with whipped cream and coarsely grated Kake Brand.

As an alternative chopped up pear halves may be placed in the bottom of each individual dish before pouring in the mousse.

Chocolate Chip Steamed Pudding

4 oz (125 g) margarine
4 oz (125 g) caster or soft brown sugar
4 oz (125 g) self raising flour
Pinch of salt
2 eggs, well beaten
2 tablespoons (2×15 ml) milk
A few drops vanilla essence
2 oz (50 g) Kake Brand (milk or plain), coarsely grated

Cream margarine and sugar until light and fluffy. Sift flour and salt. Add beaten eggs and flour alternately to the creamed mixture. Add milk and vanilla essence and beat well. Finally fold in the Kake Brand.

Spoon into a well greased pudding basin 1½–2 pint (1 litre) size. Cover with a double thickness of well greased greaseproof paper and tie securely. Steam for 1½ hours.

Serve with custard sauce or, if liked, this pudding is delicious served with Chocolate Orange and Walnut Sauce (see page 61).

Old Farmhouse Chocolate Pudding

4 oz (125 g) Kake Brand (milk or plain), roughly chopped
¼ pint (150 ml) milk
3 oz (75 g) margarine
4 oz (125 g) caster sugar
2 eggs, separated
½ teaspoon (2.5 ml) vanilla essence
6 oz (175 g) white breadcrumbs

Melt Kake Brand over hot but not boiling water, add the milk and stir well. Cream margarine and sugar together until light and fluffy. Beat in the egg yolks and vanilla essence. Add the breadcrumbs alternately with the chocolate milk, beating well after each addition. Beat egg whites until stiff and fold into the mixture.

Pour into a well greased pudding basin 1½–2 pint (1 litre) size. Cover with a double thickness of well greased greaseproof paper. Tie securely and steam for 1 hour.

Serve with custard sauce or Chocolate Ginger Sauce (see page 60).

Hot Chocolate Soufflé

1 oz (25 g) margarine
1 oz (25 g) plain flour
¼ pint (150 ml) milk
1 oz (25 g) caster sugar
2 oz (50 g) Kake Brand (milk or plain), coarsely grated
3 eggs, separated
A few drops vanilla essence

Put margarine and flour into a saucepan, stir over a low heat until margarine has melted and is well mixed with the flour. Cook and stir for 1 minute. Remove from heat and gradually add the milk, stirring well after each addition to avoid lumps.

Return to the heat and bring to the boil, stirring all the time. Cook for 3 minutes. Remove from heat and beat in sugar and grated Kake Brand. Allow to cool slightly then add the egg yolks and vanilla, beating well after each addition. Beat the egg whites until stiff then fold into the mixture. Pour into a greased soufflé dish or deep pie dish, 1½ pint (¾ litre) size.

Bake in a moderately hot oven 350°F/180°C/Gas Mark 4 for 40 minutes. Dredge with caster sugar and serve immediately with whipped cream.

Chocolate Rice Pudding

2 oz (50 g) Kake Brand (milk or plain), coarsely grated
1 pint (600 ml) milk
2 oz (50 g) pudding rice
1 oz (25 g) caster sugar
½ teaspoon (2.5 ml) vanilla essence
½ oz (15 g) butter

Melt the Kake Brand over hot but not boiling water, then whisk into milk. Wash rice and drain well. Put into a well greased ovenproof dish—1½ pint (¾ litre) size. Add milk, sugar and vanilla. Stir well. Dot with butter.

Bake in a slow oven 300°F/150°C/Gas Mark 2 for 2–2½ hours. Stir two or three times during the first hour to increase creaminess.

Austrian Chocolate Pudding

2½ oz (65 g) Kake Brand (milk or plain), roughly chopped
4 eggs, separated
2½ oz (65 g) butter or luxury margarine
2½ oz (65 g) caster sugar
2½ oz (65 g) ground almonds

Melt Kake Brand over hot but not boiling water. Beat egg yolks and mix with melted Kake Brand. Beat egg whites until stiff. Cream butter or margarine and sugar until light and fluffy. Beat in egg yolks and Kake Brand. Fold in stiffly beaten egg whites alternately with the ground almonds.

Spoon mixture into a well greased pudding basin 1½–2 pint (1 litre) size. Cover with a double thickness of well greased greaseproof paper and tie securely. Steam for 1–1¼ hours.

Serve with Chocolate and Spiced Rum Sauce (see page 61) and whipped cream, if liked.

COLD SWEETS FOR SPECIAL OCCASIONS

Entertaining family and friends is for most of us a real joy, marred only occasionally by the anxiety of what to serve for dessert. We all like to find something new, and we all enjoy being complimented on our efforts. Browse through this chapter and I'm sure you will find the perfect sweet to complement your other courses.

Some can be prepared quickly, and most can be prepared a day in advance, leaving you free on the special day to concentrate on other things. I'm sure everyone will really enjoy these delicious chocolate desserts.

Scrumptious Mocha Pie

For the pie base
1½ oz (40 g) butter *or* luxury margarine
¾ oz (20 g) caster sugar
2 oz (50 g) Kake Brand (milk *or* plain), roughly chopped
3 oz (75 g) biscuit crumbs
For the filling
1 litre coffee *or* chocolate ice cream
2 oz (50 g) plain Kake Brand, roughly chopped
3 oz (75 g) soft brown sugar
1 oz (25 g) butter
1 6 oz (175 g) tin evaporated milk
For the topping
1 tablespoon (15 ml) Kahlua liqueur *or* Tia Maria liqueur
5 fl oz (150 ml) sweetened whipped cream
2 oz (50 g) chopped nuts

Melt butter or margarine and sugar in a saucepan over a gentle heat. Melt Kake Brand over hot but not boiling water. Add biscuit crumbs to melted mixture. Mix well, then stir in Kake Brand. Spoon mixture into a fairly deep 8 in. (20 cm) pie plate. Press evenly to cover bottom and sides. Allow to set for about 30 minutes.

To prepare filling, spoon ice cream on to base, level off and put into freezer or ice box of refrigerator. Put Kake Brand into a fairly large bowl and allow to melt over hot but not boiling water. Stir in sugar and butter, then slowly add the evaporated milk. Cook over hot water until thick. Remove from heat, allow to cool, then chill. Spread chocolate mixture over ice cream and return to ice box or freezer.

Just before serving add liqueur to sweetened whipped cream. Spoon or pipe on top of pie. Sprinkle with chopped nuts.

Oregon Chocolate Soufflé

½ oz (15 g) gelatine
2 tablespoons (2×15 ml) cold water
3 tablespoons (3×15 ml) crème-de-cacao
4 oz (125 g) soft brown sugar
6 oz (175 g) plain Kake Brand, roughly chopped
4 eggs, separated
Pinch of salt
5 fl oz (150 ml) whipped cream
For the decoration
5 fl oz (150 ml) sweetened whipped cream
2 oz (50 g) finely chopped pistachio nuts *or* walnuts

Put gelatine, water, crème-de-cacao and half the brown sugar into a fairly large saucepan. Stir constantly over a low heat until gelatine and sugar are dissolved. Add Kake Brand and stir until melted. Remove from heat and beat in the egg yolks, one at a time. Allow to cool. Add salt to egg whites, beat until stiff but not dry. Beat in the remaining sugar, and continue beating until very stiff. Fold egg white mixture into the cooled gelatine mixture. Fold in the whipped cream.

Tie a double band of greaseproof paper round a 2 pint (1.2 l) soufflé dish, allowing sufficient height for the paper to come at least 2 in. (5 cm) above the rim. Grease the dish and paper very lightly. Pour the mixture into the dish and leave to set overnight in the refrigerator. Before serving, carefully remove the paper band. Decorate with whipped cream and chopped nuts.

Chocolate Dessert Cups

6 oz (175 g) Kake Brand (milk or plain), roughly chopped
½ oz (15 g) butter
3 eggs, separated
1 tablespoon (15 ml) black rum
1 tablespoon (15 ml) very strong black coffee
Whipped cream and chocolate curls and toasted coconut for decoration

Put Kake Brand and butter into a large bowl and melt over hot but not boiling water. Beat egg yolks until light and creamy, and add to melted Kake Brand. Beat in the rum and coffee. Beat egg whites until very stiff and fold into chocolate mixture. Pour into individual glasses. Sprinkle with toasted coconut and leave to set. Decorate with whipped cream and chocolate curls. Chill well before serving.

Chocolate Chalet Gâteau

8 oz (225 g) Kake Brand (milk or plain), roughly chopped
2 oz (50 g) butter or luxury margarine
2 tablespoons (2×15 ml) golden syrup
1 teaspoon (5 ml) ground cinnamon
Finely grated rind of one orange or one lemon
3 eggs
12 oz (350 g) broken biscuits
¼ pint (150 ml) double or whipping cream
¼ pint (150 ml) single or pouring cream
1 tablespoon (15 ml) orange curacao liqueur or cherry brandy (optional)
1 oz (25 g) Kake Brand (milk or plain), coarsely grated.

Put 8 oz (225 g) Kake Brand, butter, syrup, cinnamon and finely grated rind into a large bowl and melt over hot but not boiling water. Remove from heat and beat in the eggs, one at a time. Add broken biscuits and mix well. Spoon mixture into a lightly greased 7 in. (18 cm) square or 8 in. (20 cm) round sponge tin. Press well into tin, and if liked the surface may be rubbed all over with the cut side of an orange or lemon. Cover with foil or cling film and leave to set in the refrigerator for at least 2 hours or over night.

Remove cake from tin by running a hot palette knife round sides, and hold base in hot water for one minute. Place on serving dish, mix double and single cream, add liqueur if used, and whisk until cream stands in soft peaks. Spoon over top and sides of cake, then sprinkle with coarsely grated Kake Brand. Serve well chilled cut in slices or wedges.

Chocolate Belgravia

2 oz (50 g) Kake Brand (milk or plain), roughly chopped
1 tablespoon (15 ml) cold water
2 eggs, separated
8 sponge finger biscuits
1 tin (11 oz/300 g) mandarin orange segments
1 tablespoon (15 ml) sherry or brandy
A few drops vanilla essence
1 tablespoon (15 ml) caster sugar
Angelica

Put Kake Brand and water into a large bowl and melt over hot but not boiling water. Add well beaten egg yolks to the chocolate mixture, whisk and cook for 5 minutes until thick.

Remove from heat. Place sponge fingers in shallow heatproof dish. Drain fruit, mix juice with sherry or brandy and pour over sponge fingers. Spoon fruit on top reserving a few segments for decoration. Pour over the chocolate mixture. Beat egg whites with the vanilla essence until stiff. Beat in half the sugar.

Spoon meringue over the chocolate mixture, sprinkle with the remaining sugar. Decorate with orange segments and angelica leaves. Place under a hot grill until meringue is golden brown. Chocolate Belgravia may be served immediately or left to cool if desired.

Oregon Chocolate Soufflé, Chocolate Chalet Gâteau, Chocolate Belgravia.

Raspberry or Pear Meringue Gâteau

For the meringue
3 egg whites
6 oz (175 g) icing sugar
For the filling
6 oz (175 g) Kake Brand (milk or plain), roughly chopped
¼ pint (150 ml) double or whipping cream
¼ pint (150 ml) single or pouring cream
1 oz (25 g) caster sugar
1 tin (15 oz/425 g) pear halves or 8 oz (225 g) fresh or frozen raspberries

First line the bottoms of two baking trays with greaseproof paper. Using a round 7 in. (18 cm) sponge tin as a guide draw two circles on one tray and one circle on the other. Grease the paper well, then hold the paper under cold running water for approximately 10 seconds, shake off any surplus water and return to tray. Half fill a saucepan with water and bring to the boil. Remove from heat. Put egg whites into a bowl which fits well over the pan of water. Add sifted sugar. Place bowl on top of pan and whisk mixture until very thick, or until whisk leaves a trail across the top when lifted. Remove bowl from saucepan and continue whisking until mixture is cool.

Spoon mixture evenly within the three circles and with a round bladed knife smooth the surface. Bake in a very cool oven 225°F/110°C/Gas Mark ¼ for 3½−4 hours. When meringue circles are cooked they should easily lift off the greaseproof paper. Remove from oven and allow to become cold.

Melt Kake Brand over hot but not boiling water. Turn circles of meringue upside down and coat each one with melted Kake Brand. Allow to harden. Whip creams and caster sugar together until cream stands in soft peaks. Drain syrup from pears, if used, and roughly chop. Set aside a few pieces of pear or several of the most perfect raspberries for decoration. Carefully fold in the remainder of the raspberries or pears to the cream.

Put one layer of meringue on to a large round serving plate, chocolate side down. Spread with half the cream mixture, cover with another meringue layer, chocolate side down, and spread with remainder of the cream. Top with final layer of meringue, chocolate side down.

Decorate the top of this delicious gâteau with whipped cream rosettes (using a No. 6 or No. 8 star nozzle), and the raspberries or chopped pears.

Chocolate Pavlova

For the meringue
4 egg whites
Pinch of salt
8 oz (225 g) caster sugar
½ teaspoon (2.5 ml) ground cinnamon
1 teaspoon (5 ml) vinegar
For the chocolate filling
6 oz (175 g) Kake Brand (milk or plain), roughly chopped
3 tablespoons (3×15 ml) cold water
4 well beaten egg yolks
For the topping
¼ pint (150 ml) whipping cream
1 tablespoon (15 ml) caster sugar
½ teaspoon (2.5 ml) ground cinnamon
1 oz (25 g) Kake Brand (milk or plain), coarsely grated

First line the bottom of a baking tray with greaseproof paper. Using a round 8 in. (20 cm) sponge tin as a guide, draw a circle. Grease the paper well then hold the paper under cold running water for approximately 10 seconds, shake off any surplus water and return to tray. Whisk the egg whites with the salt until very stiff. Add sugar, cinnamon and vinegar and carefully fold into the beaten egg whites. Spoon mixture on to prepared paper and spread neatly to form a round cake within the circle approximately 2 in. (5 cm) thick.

Sprinkle top and sides with caster sugar and bake as follows. With electric cookers bake at 325°F/170°C for 55 minutes. Switch off and leave in oven for a further 35 minutes. With gas cookers bake at Gas Mark 1 for 55 minutes then reduce to setting ½ for 35 minutes.

Remove from oven, turn upside down on to a large 9–10 in. (23–25 cm) plate and remove paper.

To prepare chocolate filling, put Kake Brand and water into a fairly large bowl and allow to melt over hot but not boiling water. Add the well beaten egg yolks and cook and stir until the mixture thickens. Remove from heat, allow to cool slightly and spoon over Pavlova.

To prepare topping, whip cream, caster sugar and cinnamon together until cream stands in soft peaks. Spoon over chocolate filling and decorate with coarsely grated Kake Brand. Chill well before serving.

Pots-au-Chocolat

4 oz (125 g) Kake Brand (milk or plain), roughly chopped
1 oz (25 g) butter
2 eggs, separated
4 oz (125 g) white marshmallows
1 tablespoon (15 ml) hot water
Whipped cream and chocolate curls for decoration

Put Kake Brand and butter into a large bowl and melt over hot but not boiling water. Add well beaten egg yolks and marshmallows. Cook, stirring occasionally till mixture melts and is smooth and shiny. Add water and mix well. Remove from heat. Beat egg whites until very stiff and fold into mixture. Pour into individual glasses and chill well. Just before serving decorate with whipped cream and chocolate curls.

Chocolate Pavlova, Pots-au-Chocolat.

SAUCES, SPREADS, FILLINGS AND FROSTINGS

Hot Chocolate Sauce (with variations)

2 oz (50 g) Kake Brand (milk or plain), roughly chopped
½ oz (15 g) butter or luxury margarine
2 tablespoons (2×15 ml) milk or water

Put all ingredients into a small bowl and allow to melt over hot but not boiling water. Stir well.

Hot Chocolate Sauce is a real "family favourite" to serve with ice cream. The variations are numerous, and there is one to suit every taste and occasion.

Variations
Chocolate Orange
Add grated rind of one orange. Substitute 1 tablespoon (15 ml) orange juice for 1 tablespoon (15 ml) milk or water.
Chocolate Honey
Add 2 teaspoons (2×5 ml) honey and 1 teaspoon (5 ml) lemon juice.
Mocha
Substitute very strong black coffee for milk and water.
Chocolate Peanut
Add 2 oz (50 g) chopped salted peanuts.
Chocolate Rum
Add 2 teaspoons (2×5 ml) black rum.
Chocolate Coconut
Add 2 oz (50 g) coconut.
Chocolate Ginger
Add 1 oz (25 g) chopped crystallised or stem ginger.

Chocolate Sauce

3 oz (75 g) caster sugar
4 fl oz (125 ml) cold water
2 oz (50 g) plain Kake Brand, roughly chopped
Knob of butter

Dissolve sugar in water over a gentle heat. Bring to the boil, and boil for 3–4 minutes. Reduce heat. Add Kake Brand and cook gently till smooth, stirring all the time. Add butter and beat well.

This sauce may be served hot with ice cream. To use cold, pour into a bowl or container, cover and store in the refrigerator until required. It is delicious cold served with cream filled profiteroles.

Note: If chocolate sauce turns sugary on cooling, add a teaspoon (5 ml) of boiling water and stir until smooth.

Chocolate Orange and Walnut Sauce

4 oz (125 g) Kake Brand (milk *or* plain), roughly chopped
4 tablespoons (4×15 ml) orange juice *or* undiluted orange squash
Knob of butter
2 oz (50 g) chopped walnuts

Put Kake Brand, orange juice and butter into a bowl and allow to melt over hot but not boiling water. Stir well and add chopped nuts.

Chocolate and Spiced Rum Sauce

4 oz (125 g) Kake Brand (milk *or* plain), roughly chopped
2 tablespoons (2×15 ml) milk
2 tablespoons (2×15 ml) black rum
Knob of butter
Pinch of cinnamon

Put Kake Brand into a small bowl and allow to melt over hot but not boiling water. Add milk, rum, butter and cinnamon. Stir and heat gently.

These two sauces are delicious served with steamed puddings or ice cream.

Dreamy Chocolate Cream

2 oz (50 g) cornflour
¼ pint (150 ml) evaporated milk *plus* ¼ pint (150 ml) cold water *or* ½ pint (300 ml) milk
4 oz (125 g) Kake Brand (milk *or* plain), roughly chopped
3 oz (75 g) butter *or* luxury margarine
2 oz (50 g) caster sugar

Blend cornflour with a little of the milk and water. Warm the remainder and pour over the cornflour. Return to the heat and stir until thick. Stir and cook for 2 minutes. Cover and leave to cool. Melt the Kake Brand over hot but not boiling water. Beat butter and sugar together until really light and fluffy, then gradually beat in the cooled cornflour and melted Kake Brand. Continue beating until mixture is the consistency of thick whipped cream.

Use as a filling or topping for cakes. It pipes very well.

Rich Chocolate Butter Cream Filling

4 tablespoons (4×15 ml) cold water
2 oz (50 g) caster sugar
2 egg yolks, well beaten
6 oz (175 g) butter *or* luxury margarine
2 oz (50 g) Kake Brand (milk *or* plain), roughly chopped

Dissolve sugar in water and boil until syrup forms a short thread between the thumb and first finger when tested. Pour syrup very slowly on to the egg yolks, beating all the time. Allow to cool. Cream butter until very soft and fluffy, then gradually beat in the egg yolk mixture. Melt the Kake Brand over hot but not boiling water, and beat in.

Use as a filling or topping for cakes. It is excellent for piping.

Chocolate Orange and Walnut Sauce and Chocolate Chip Steamed Pudding, Austrian Chocolate Pudding, Chocolate and Spiced Rum Sauce.

American Chocolate Frosting

3 oz (75 g) Kake Brand (milk or plain), roughly chopped
6 oz (175 g) butter or luxury margarine
4 oz (125 g) sifted icing sugar
3 eggs, separated

Put Kake Brand into a bowl and melt over hot but not boiling water. Cream butter and sugar together until very light and fluffy. Add egg yolks, one at a time, beating very well after each addition. Slowly beat in the melted Kake Brand. Whisk egg whites until very stiff and fold into the mixture.

Use this frosting to sandwich and coat layer cakes of at least 8 in. (20 cm) in diameter.

Chocolate Butter Cream Filling

3 oz (75 g) Kake Brand (milk or plain), roughly chopped
3 oz (75 g) butter or luxury margarine
5 oz (150 g) sifted icing sugar

Melt Kake Brand over hot but not boiling water. Cream butter and sugar together until light and very fluffy. Slowly beat in the melted Kake Brand.

Use as a filling or topping for cakes.

Very Special Chocolate Cream

¼ pint (150 ml) milk
8 oz (225 g) Kake Brand (milk or plain), coarsely grated
or
¼ pint (150 ml) double or whipping cream
5 oz (150 ml) Kake Brand (milk or plain), coarsely grated

Bring milk or cream to boiling point but do not boil. Pour on to Kake Brand and leave to cool. If a piping consistency is needed, beat well. This quantity will fill and cover a 7 in. (18 cm) diameter cake.

TRAY BAKES

How many times do you hear the phrase "I would love to do more home-baking, but I just don't have the time"? I'm quite certain that you have the odd hour when you could shut yourself in the kitchen and really enjoy trying out these Tray Bakes. All the recipes are fairly easy and all are quick to prepare—you can't really go wrong. They're ideal family bakes and all store well in airtight containers, if they are allowed to! They're great too for contributions to cake and candy stalls, coffee mornings, etc.

Fudgy Brownies

4 oz (125 g) Kake Brand (milk or plain), roughly chopped
6 oz (175 g) butter or luxury margarine
12 oz (350 g) caster sugar
3 beaten eggs
1 teaspoon (5 ml) vanilla essence
3 oz (75 g) chopped walnuts (if liked)
6 oz (175 g) self raising flour
Pinch of salt

Place roughly chopped Kake Brand and butter or margarine in a large bowl and melt over hot but not boiling water. Remove from heat. Add sugar, beaten eggs and vanilla essence. Mix well. Stir in walnuts. Gradually add sifted flour and salt, mixing very well. Pour mixture into a well greased oblong tin, approximately 13×9×2 in. (33×23×5 cm) and bake in a moderately hot oven 350°F/180°C/Gas Mark 4 for 45–50 minutes. Allow to become quite cold before cutting into squares or fingers.

Toffee Nut Bars

6 oz (175 g) butter *or* luxury margarine
3 oz (75 g) caster sugar
3 oz (75 g) dark soft brown sugar
1 beaten egg yolk
1 teaspoon (5 ml) vanilla essence
5 oz (150 g) plain flour
5 oz (150 g) self raising flour
Pinch of salt
8 oz (225 g) Kake Brand (milk *or* plain)
2 oz (50 g) chopped walnuts *or* hazelnuts

Cream butter or margarine with the sugar until light and fluffy. Beat in egg yolk and vanilla essence. Sift flour and salt and gradually add to creamed mixture, mixing well. Spoon mixture on to a well greased baking tray 13×9 in. (33×23 cm) and spread evenly. Bake in a moderately hot oven 350°F/180°C/Gas Mark 4 for 25–30 minutes until lightly browned.

Allow the mixture to cool for 10 minutes and then cover with melted Kake Brand and sprinkle with chopped nuts. Cut into squares or fingers just as the Kake Brand is beginning to harden. Cool completely on a wire tray before storing in an airtight container.

Date and Nut Crunchy Bars

For the base
4 oz (125 g) finely crushed cornflakes *or* 3 oz (75 g) finely crushed cornflakes *plus* 1 oz (25 g) finely crushed All-Bran
3 oz (75 g) butter *or* luxury margarine
2 oz (50 g) caster sugar
For the topping
6 oz (175 g) Kake Brand (milk *or* plain), roughly chopped
1 oz (25 g) butter *or* luxury margarine
4 oz (125 g) finely chopped dates
2 oz (50 g) chopped walnuts *or* peanuts
A few drops vanilla essence

Fruity Chocolate Squares, Simple Florentines, Date and Nut Crunchy Bars, Toffee Nut Bars, Millionaire's Shortbread, Date and Nut Crunchy Bars, Chocolate Mint Fingers, Coconut Delight.

67

Place cornflakes in a bowl, add butter or margarine which has been cut into small pieces and rub in. Add caster sugar and mix well. Spoon mixture into a well greased oblong tin 11×7×1½ in. (28×18×4 cm), and spread evenly. Bake in a fairly hot oven 375°F/190°C/Gas Mark 5 for 15 minutes. Allow to cool.

Place roughly chopped Kake Brand and butter or margarine in a bowl and allow to melt over hot but not boiling water. Stir in dates, nuts and vanilla essence. Spread evenly over base and when topping is beginning to harden, score roughly with the prongs of a fork. When completely hardened cut into fingers or squares.

Coconut Delight

6 oz (175 g) Kake Brand (milk or plain), roughly chopped
2 eggs
4 oz (125 g) caster sugar
6 oz (175 g) coconut, as rough as possible
2 oz (50 g) chopped cherries
2 oz (50 g) chopped crystallised ginger (if liked)

Melt the Kake Brand over hot but not boiling water. Pour into an oblong tin 11×7 in. (28×18 cm) and spread evenly. Allow to harden. Place eggs and sugar in a bowl and beat well. Add coconut, cherries and ginger, if used, and mix well. Pour on top of Kake Brand, spread evenly and bake in a moderately hot oven 350°F/180°C/Gas Mark 4 for 20–25 minutes. Allow to cool completely before cutting into fingers or squares.

Crunchy Crunchies

5 oz (150 g) self raising flour
Pinch of salt
1 teaspoon (5 ml) baking powder
3 oz (75 g) coconut
2 oz (50 g) crushed cornflakes
2 oz (50 g) caster sugar
4 oz (125 g) margarine
6 oz (175 g) Kake Brand (milk or plain), roughly chopped

Sift, flour, salt and baking powder into a bowl, add coconut, crushed cornflakes and sugar and mix well. Place margarine in saucepan and melt slowly. Make a hollow in centre of dry ingredients and pour in melted margarine. Mix together with a fork. This will be a crumbly mixture. Spoon mixture into a greased baking tray, 13×9 in. (33×23 cm) and spread evenly. Bake in a fairly hot oven 375°F/190°C/Gas Mark 5 for 15 minutes until golden brown.

Allow to cool for 5 minutes. Melt Kake Brand over hot but not boiling water, and pour over crunchy base, spreading evenly. When Kake Brand has hardened cut into squares or fingers.

Millionaire's Shortbread

For the shortbread base
6 oz (175 g) self raising flour
Pinch of salt
4 oz (125 g) butter or luxury margarine
2 oz (50 g) caster sugar
For the filling
4 oz (125 g) margarine
4 oz (125 g) caster sugar
2 tablespoons (2×15 ml) golden syrup
1 small tin (7 oz/200 g) sweetened condensed milk
6 oz (175 g) Kake Brand (milk or plain), roughly chopped

Sift flour and salt into a bowl, add butter or margarine which has been cut into small pieces. Rub into flour until mixture resembles fine breadcrumbs. Add sugar and mix well. Spoon mixture into a greased oblong tray 11×7 in. (28×18 cm) and spread evenly. Bake in a moderately hot oven 350°F/180°C/Gas Mark 4 for 20 minutes. Leave to cool.

Melt margarine, sugar and syrup in a saucepan, add condensed milk and boil for 6 minutes stirring all the time. Pour evenly over the shortbread base and allow to cool. Melt Kake Brand over hot but not boiling water and pour over filling, and allow to harden before cutting into fingers or squares.

Fruity Chocolate Squares

4 oz (125 g) margarine
4 oz (125 g) caster sugar
4 oz (125 g) self raising flour
Pinch of salt
2 beaten eggs
A few drops vanilla essence
2 oz (50 g) Kake Brand (milk or plain)
2 oz (50 g) chopped raisins
2 oz (50 g) chopped walnuts or peanuts

Cream margarine and sugar until light and fluffy. Sift flour and salt and add alternately with the beaten egg and vanilla, to the creamed mixture, beating well after each addition. Melt the Kake Brand over hot but not boiling water, and add to mixture. Finally add chopped raisins and nuts and stir evenly through the mixture.

Turn mixture into an oblong tin 11×7×2 in. (28×18×5 cm) which has been greased and lined with greaseproof paper. Bake in a moderately hot oven 350°F/180°C/Gas Mark 4 for 30 minutes or until cooked. Remove from oven and immediately sprinkle with caster sugar. Cool on a wire tray and cut into squares when cold.

These squares keep very well in an airtight container.

Chocolate Mint Fingers

For the base
4 oz (125 g) self raising flour
Pinch of salt
1 teaspoon (5 ml) baking powder
1 tablespoon (15 ml) cocoa
4 oz (125 g) luxury margarine
2 oz (50 g) dark soft brown sugar
3 oz (75 g) crushed cornflakes
For the filling
2 egg whites
12 oz (350 g) icing sugar
1 teaspoon (5 ml) peppermint essence *or* 5 drops of oil of peppermint
Few drops of green colouring
For the topping
6 oz (175 g) Kake Brand (milk or plain), roughly chopped

Sift flour, salt, baking powder and cocoa into a bowl, add margarine cut into small pieces and rub into flour until mixture resembles fine breadcrumbs. Add sugar and crushed cornflakes. Spoon on to a well greased baking tray approximately 13×9 in. (33×23 cm) and spread out with a round bladed knife. Bake in a slow oven 300°F/150°C/Gas Mark 2 for 20 minutes.

Beat egg whites until frothy, add sifted icing sugar and peppermint essence and beat until smooth. Adjust peppermint flavour if required, to personal taste. Carefully add green colouring until filling turns to a pale peppermint green colour. Spread over the cool base.

Melt the roughly chopped Kake Brand over hot but not boiling water. Pour over filling and spread evenly. Cut into fingers when Kake Brand is almost hard.

Fudgy Chocolate Fingers

4 oz (125 g) butter or luxury margarine
6 oz (175 g) demerara sugar
2 rounded tablespoons (4×15 ml) golden syrup
1 small tin (7 oz/200 g) sweetened full cream condensed milk
8 oz (225 g) crushed digestive biscuits
6 oz (175 g) Kake Brand (milk or plain), roughly chopped

Put butter, sugar, syrup and condensed milk into a saucepan and melt over a low heat stirring all the time. Bring to a gentle boil and cook for 6 minutes. Remove from heat and beat well. Add crushed biscuits and mix well. Spoon into a well greased baking tray approximately 12×8 in. (30×20 cm) and spread evenly with a round bladed knife.

Melt roughly chopped Kake Brand over hot but not boiling water. Pour over base, spread evenly and cut into fingers when Kake Brand is almost hard.

Viennese Biscuit Cake

2 oz (50 g) butter or luxury margarine
2 tablespoons (2×15 ml) golden syrup
5 oz (150 g) Kake Brand (milk or plain), coarsely grated
8 oz (225 g) crushed digestive biscuits

Melt together in a fairly large saucepan over a gentle heat, the butter, syrup and Kake Brand. Remove from heat, add the crushed biscuits and mix well until mixture forms a smooth paste.

Spoon into a well greased 7–8 in. (18–20 cm) fluted flan ring or round sponge tin. Smooth the surface by pressing the cut side of a lemon or orange over all. Allow to become quite cold before removing from ring or tin. Decorate if liked, with Chocolate Butter Cream (see page 64).

Simple Florentines

For the base
2 oz (50 g) butter or luxury margarine
1 tablespoon (15 ml) clear honey
2 oz (50 g) finely chopped dates
2 oz (50 g) chopped raisins or sultanas
2 oz (50 g) chopped glacé cherries
2 oz (50 g) chopped walnuts
2 oz (50 g) coarsely crushed wheatflakes or Rice Krispies
For the topping
6 oz (175 g) Kake Brand (milk or plain), roughly chopped
2 tablespoons (2×15 ml) milk

Melt butter and honey over a low heat. Add dates and cook for one minute, stirring constantly. Remove from heat, stir in raisins, cherries, nuts and wheatflakes or Rice Krispies. Mix well. Spoon mixture on to a well greased oblong tray approximately 11×7×2 in. (28×18×5 cm), spread evenly with a round bladed knife. Allow to cool.

Melt Kake Brand and milk in a basin over hot but not boiling water, stirring frequently. Pour over base and allow to become quite cold before cutting into squares, bars or fingers.

Chewy Chocolate Squares

2 oz (50 g) Kake Brand (milk or plain), roughly chopped
2 eggs
6 oz (175 g) caster sugar
1 teaspoon (5 ml) vanilla essence
4 tablespoons (4×15 ml) cooking oil
5 oz (150 g) plain flour
½ teaspoon (2.5 ml) salt
1 rounded teaspoon (2×5 ml) baking powder
2 oz (50 g) chopped walnuts or hazelnuts

Place roughly chopped Kake Brand in a small bowl and melt over hot but not boiling water. Break eggs into a bowl and add caster sugar and vanilla essence, whisk until fluffy. Mix in oil and melted Kake Brand. Sift flour, salt and baking powder and fold into mixture. Finally add chopped nuts.

Pour mixture into a well greased and lined oblong tin, 11×7×2 in. (28×18×5 cm) and bake in a moderately hot oven 350°F/180°C/Gas Mark 4 for 30 minutes. Cool for 10 minutes, then cut into squares. Remove from tin on to a wire cooling tray.

Raisin Bars

For the bars
2 oz (50 g) butter or luxury margarine
2 tablespoons (2×15 ml) golden syrup
Finely grated rind of one orange
4 oz (125 g) raisins
2 oz (50 g) finely chopped mixed peel
8 oz (225 g) crushed digestive biscuits
For the chocolate glacé icing
4 oz (125 g) Kake Brand (milk or plain), coarsely grated
4 oz (125 g) icing sugar
1 tablespoon (15 ml) water
A few drops vanilla essence

Melt butter and syrup in a large pan over gentle heat. Add orange rind, raisins and mixed peel and cook for one minute. Remove from heat and add biscuit crumbs. Mix well together. Spoon on to a well greased oblong tray approximately 12×8×1½ in. (30×20×4 cm), spread evenly with a round bladed knife and leave to harden.

Put grated Kake Brand into a saucepan, add sifted icing sugar, water and vanilla essence. Stir over a low heat until Kake Brand has melted. Do not allow to boil. Pour over base and spread evenly. When icing has set cut in fingers or squares.

BISCUITS

Everyone loves home-made biscuits. They're easy to make and so economical. If you are a newcomer to home baking here are a few hints which will help.

If liquid is added do this carefully as too much will make the dough soft, sticky and difficult to handle. Biscuits are usually cooked near the top of a fairly hot oven. Keep a watchful eye on them, particularly chocolate ones as they brown quickly. Remove from the oven as soon as they are evenly browned. Cool on a wire tray and store in an airtight container.

Crunchy Cookies

2 oz (50 g) plain flour *plus* 1 teaspoon (5 ml) baking powder *or* 2 oz (50 g) self raising flour
Pinch of salt
1 oz (25 g) semolina or farola
2 oz (50 g) rolled oats
2 oz (50 g) caster sugar
2 oz (50 g) vegetable fat shortening
2 tablespoons (2×15 ml) golden syrup
¼ teaspoon (1.25 ml) bicarbonate of soda
1 teaspoon (5 ml) milk
2 oz (50 g) Kake Brand (milk or plain), roughly chopped

Sift flour, baking powder if used, salt, semolina or farola, into a bowl and add the rolled oats. Put the sugar, vegetable fat shortening and syrup into a pan and heat until melted. Add the melted mixture to the dry ingredients and mix well. Dissolve the bicarbonate of soda in the milk and stir in together with the roughly chopped Kake Brand.

Roll into small balls the size of a shelled walnut and place fairly well apart on greased baking trays. Bake near the top of a fairly hot oven 375°F/190°C/Gas Mark 5 for 12–15 minutes. Cool on a wire tray. These biscuits, if liked, can be decorated with pieces of glacé cherry or flaked almonds placed in centre before baking.

Makes approximately 30 biscuits.

Disneyland Cookies

4 oz (125 g) self raising flour
Pinch of salt
2 oz (50 g) creamy white vegetable fat shortening
4 oz (125 g) demerara sugar
6 oz (175 g) Kake Brand (milk or plain), coarsely grated
2 oz (50 g) chopped nuts (walnuts, almonds, hazelnuts)
1 beaten egg
½ teaspoon (2.5 ml) vanilla essence

Sift flour and salt into a bowl and add all other ingredients. Cream together with a wooden spoon for one minute. Roll into balls about the size of a shelled walnut and place fairly well apart on greased baking trays.

Bake near the top of a fairly hot oven 375°F/190°C/Gas Mark 5 for 12–15 minutes until golden brown. Lift on to a wire tray to cool.

Makes approximately 48 cookies.

Carolina Cookies

1 beaten egg
6 oz (175 g) granulated sugar
3 oz (75 g) butter or luxury margarine
4 oz (125 g) Kake Brand (milk or plain), roughly chopped
6 oz (175 g) self raising flour
Pinch of salt

Beat egg and sugar together for about 2 minutes using a rotary beater (1 minute using a food mixer). Add butter or margarine which has been melted with the Kake Brand over hot but not boiling water. Stir in flour and salt. Roll into small walnut size balls. Place well apart on greased baking trays. Bake at 400°F/200°C/Gas Mark 6 for approximately 10 minutes.

Makes 60 biscuits.

Danish Cookies

6 oz (175 g) plain flour
Pinch of salt
5 oz (150 g) margarine
3 oz (75 g) icing sugar
2 oz (50 g) Kake Brand (milk or plain), roughly chopped
1 beaten egg
2 oz (50 g) desiccated coconut
Small pieces of glacé cherry for decoration

Sift flour and salt into a bowl. Add margarine cut into small pieces and rub into flour until mixture resembles fine breadcrumbs. Add sugar, chopped Kake Brand and coconut. Mix well. Make a hollow in centre and pour in beaten egg. Mix thoroughly. Drop teaspoons or 5 ml spoons of mixture on to greased baking trays, spaced fairly well apart. Decorate each with a small piece of glacé cherry.

Bake in a fairly hot oven 375°F/190°C/Gas Mark 5 for approximately 15 minutes until golden brown. Cool on a wire tray.

Makes approximately 48 cookies.

Spicy Ice Box Cookies

8 oz (225 g) plain flour
Pinch of salt
1 teaspoon (5 ml) baking powder
2 teaspoons (2×5 ml) mixed spice
4 oz (125 g) butter or luxury margarine
6 oz (175 g) caster sugar
2 oz (50 g) finely grated Kake Brand, (milk or plain)
1 beaten egg

Sift flour, salt, baking powder and mixed spice into a bowl. Add butter or margarine cut into small pieces and rub in until mixture resembles fine breadcrumbs. Add sugar and Kake Brand and mix well. Make a hollow in centre and pour in beaten egg. Mix together and knead well to form a smooth dough. Place on a lightly floured board and shape into long rolling pin shape. Carefully lift on to a long length of aluminium foil and wrap up like a parcel, twisting ends. Roll backwards and forwards to form evenly shaped roll about 2 in. (5 cm) in diameter. Place in ice box of refrigerator for at least 24 hours.

With a sharp knife, cut thin slices from roll, as many as required, place on greased baking trays and bake in a fairly hot oven, 375°F/190°C/Gas Mark 5 for 10–12 minutes. Cool on a wire tray.

The remainder of the roll can be returned to the ice box of the refrigerator until more biscuits are required. Full quantity makes approximately 60 biscuits.

Chocolate Orange Biscuits

6 oz (175 g) self raising flour
Pinch of salt
1 oz (25 g) cornflour
Grated rind of one orange
4 oz (125 g) butter or luxury margarine
4 oz (125 g) caster sugar
1 tablespoon (15 ml) beaten egg
4 oz (125 g) grated Kake Brand (milk or plain)

Sift flour, salt and cornflour into a bowl. Add finely grated orange rind. Add butter or margarine cut into small pieces and rub in until mixture resembles fine breadcrumbs. Add sugar and mix well. Make hollow in centre and pour in beaten egg. Mix together and knead well to form a smooth dough. Turn out on to a lightly floured board. Roll out to about 1/8 in. (3 mm) in thickness and cut with a plain or fluted 2 in. (5 cm) cutter. Place biscuits on a greased baking tray and bake in a fairly hot oven 375°F/190°C/Gas Mark 5 for 15–20 minutes until golden brown. Remove from oven and while still very hot sprinkle with grated Kake Bake.

Makes approximately 30 biscuits.

Viennese Shorties and Chocolate Mallows; Chocolate Orange Biscuits; Disneyland Cookies; Danish Cookies.

Chocolate Mallows

For the biscuit base
3 oz (75 g) plain flour
¼ teaspoon (1.25 ml) baking powder
Pinch of salt
1½ oz (40 g) creamy white vegetable fat shortening
2 oz (50 g) caster sugar
1 egg yolk, beaten
2 drops vanilla essence
For the marshmallow
⅓ pint (180 ml) packet table jelly *plus* 1½ tablespoons (25 ml) hot water
3 tablespoons (3×15 ml) chilled evaporated milk
6 oz (175 g) Kake Brand (milk or plain), roughly chopped
A few blanched almonds or walnuts or glacé cherries

Chill evaporated milk in refrigerator for at least two hours.

To make biscuit base, sift flour, baking powder and salt into a bowl. Cut shortening into small pieces and rub into flour until mixture resembles fine breadcrumbs. Add sugar and mix well. Make a hollow in the centre and pour in beaten egg yolk and vanilla essence. Mix to a smooth stiff dough. Turn out on to a lightly floured board, knead well and roll out to a ¼ in. (6 mm) thickness. Cut into rounds with a 2 in. (5 cm) plain or fluted cutter. Place biscuits on greased baking trays and bake in a fairly hot oven 375°F/190°C/Gas Mark 5 for 10–12 minutes. Cool on a wire tray.

To make marshmallows, dissolve ⅓ pint (180 ml) packet of table jelly in 1½ tablespoons (25 ml) hot water. Cool. Whisk the chilled evaporated milk until very thick, then quickly and very thoroughly stir in the melted jelly. Place a dessertspoonful on each biscuit and allow to set.

Melt the Kake Brand over hot but not boiling water. Stir well and pour spoonfuls over the marshmallow and biscuit to completely cover. Top each with a blanched almond, half walnut or piece of glacé cherry.

Makes 12 mallows.

Viennese Shorties

6 oz (175 g) butter or luxury margarine
2 oz (50 g) icing sugar
6 oz (175 g) plain flour
Pinch of salt
¼ teaspoon (1.25 ml) bicarbonate of soda
2 oz (50 g) custard powder
Chocolate Butter Cream (*see* page 64)
3 oz (75 g) plain Kake Brand (6 oz/175 g to dip both ends)

Cream butter or margarine with sifted icing sugar until very light and fluffy. Fold in sifted flour, salt, baking soda and custard powder. Mix until the mixture is really well blended and fairly soft. Place the mixture in a large piping bag with a No. 8 star nozzle, and pipe in 2–2½ in. (5–6 cm) lengths on to a greased baking tray, and bake in a moderately hot oven 350°F/180°C/Gas Mark 4 for 15 minutes.

As these biscuits are fairly short leave them on the tray for 5 minutes to harden, before cooling on a wire tray. Sandwich them together with Chocolate Butter Cream, then dip either one or both ends in melted plain Kake Brand. Place biscuits on a piece of waxed paper until Kake Brand has hardened.

Makes approximately 20 shorties.

Note: If you don't want to pipe this biscuit mixture, roll into small balls and place fairly well apart on greased baking trays. Press flat with prongs of a fork. Sandwich together with Chocolate Butter Cream and dip half in melted Kake Brand.

The flavour of these shorties may be varied by substituting blancmange powder for custard powder, which makes a nice change. Orange or caramel are very popular.

HOME-MADE SWEETS

Time is the one thing which we never seem to have enough of these days. We can, too, find ourselves not having enough money for luxuries such as chocolates and candies. It is surprising just how much we can save by making our own and you'll be surprised how easy it is to make these home-made sweets.

Rum Truffles

4 oz (125 g) plain Kake Brand, roughly chopped
1 egg yolk, well beaten
½ oz (15 g) butter
1 teaspoon (5 ml) evaporated milk
1 teaspoon (5 ml) black rum
1 oz (25 g) cake or biscuit crumbs
4½ oz (140 g) plain Kake Brand, finely grated

Put Kake Brand into a fairly large bowl and melt over hot but not boiling water. Remove from heat. Add egg yolk to the melted Kake Brand and beat well. Mix in all other ingredients with the exception of the finely grated Kake Brand. Beat the mixture until it becomes thick and leave aside to cool until it is stiff enough to handle. Roll into balls ½–¾ in. (1–2 cm) in diameter, then roll in grated Kake Brand. Put truffles into sweet cases.

Make chocolate curls by using a vegetable peeler to shave off curls from the flat side of a bar of Kake Brand, or if preferred chocolate may be very coarsely grated.

Chocolate Peppermint Creams

1 egg white
8 oz (225 g) sifted icing sugar
A few drops peppermint essence
Green colouring (optional)
4 oz (125 g) Kake Brand (milk or plain), roughly chopped

Whisk egg white until frothy, add icing sugar, peppermint essence and green colouring, if used. Beat to a smooth paste. Roll into small balls and flatten to the size of a 10p piece. Allow to dry out. Melt Kake Brand over hot but not boiling water. Using two cocktail sticks or a fork dip the peppermint creams into the melted Kake Brand. Shake off surplus and leave to harden on waxed paper.

Chocolate Ginger Creams

Follow recipe for Chocolate Pepperiment Creams substituting 1 teaspoon (5 ml) ground ginger in place of peppermint essence.

Raisin Bon-bons

4 oz (125 g) crunchy peanut butter
4 oz (125 g) sifted icing sugar
½ oz (15 g) butter
4 oz (125 g) chopped raisins
4 oz (125 g) Kake Brand (milk or plain), roughly chopped

Cream peanut butter, icing sugar and butter together until light and creamy. Mix in raisins. Roll into balls about ½ in. (1 cm) in diameter. Place on a piece of waxed paper and leave to set.

Melt the Kake Brand over hot but not boiling water. Using two cocktail sticks or a fork dip the raisin balls into the Kake Brand. Shake off surplus. Placed on waxed paper and allow to harden.

Tutti-frutti Chocolates

3 oz (75 g) Philadelphia Cream Cheese
10 oz (275 g) icing sugar
1 oz (25 g) glacé cherries, chopped
1 oz (25 g) angelica, chopped
1 oz (25 g) dates, chopped
1 oz (25 g) raisins, chopped
1 oz (25 g) nuts, chopped
8 oz (225 g) plain Kake Brand
Rose petals and violets for decoration

Cream the sieved icing sugar and cheese together. Add the chopped fruit and nuts to this mixture and mix well. Roll into small balls and place on the crossed wires of a cooling tray, under which is a piece of waxed paper. Melt the Kake Brand in a bowl over hot but not boiling water. With a teaspoon pour the Kake Brand over the filling. Decorate with rose petals and violets. Allow to set and place in sweet cases. The Kake Brand on the waxed paper can be melted and used again. In fact I always use this Kake Brand to make Oriental Macaroons.

Oriental Macaroons

3 oz (75 g) plain Kake Brand, roughly chopped
1 oz (25 g) chopped stem or crystallised ginger
1 oz (25 g) rough coconut

Melt the Kake Brand over hot but not boiling water, mix in the ginger and enough coconut to bind. Place small teaspoons of this on waxed paper and allow to set. Place in sweet cases.

These with the Tutti-frutti Chocolates are a good twosome, and look attractive in a presentation box.

Chocolate Ginger Balls

4 oz (125 g) plain Kake Brand, roughly chopped
2 oz (50 g) crystallised or preserved ginger

Melt the Kake Brand over hot but not boiling water. Stir in the ginger which has been either cut into very thin shreds or chopped finely. Mix until ginger is well coated with Kake Brand. Spoon into sweet cases or place in small mounds on waxed paper. Leave to harden.

After Dinner Mints

6 oz (175 g) Kake Brand (milk or plain), roughly chopped
6 oz (175 g) sifted icing sugar
A few drops oil of peppermint or ½ teaspoon (2.5 ml) peppermint essence
Hot water

Put half the Kake Brand into a small bowl and allow to melt over hot but not boiling water. Place a sheet of waxed paper on a flat board and draw a square approximately 7×7 in. (18×18 cm). With a pastry brush paint the square with melted Kake Brand. Allow to harden. Mix icing sugar and peppermint oil or essence with enough hot water to make a fairly stiff paste. Spread mixture on to Kake Brand and allow to set.

Melt the remainder of the Kake Brand and paint over the peppermint filling. Allow to harden. With a hot sharp knife cut into squares.

Chocolate Peppermint Creams, Rum Truffles and Oriental Macaroons; After Dinner Mints and Chocolate Marzipan Brazils; Tutti-frutti Chocolates; Chocolate Liqueurs.

Chocolate Liqueurs

Cocktail or maraschino cherries
Brandy
8 oz (225 g) plain Kake Brand, roughly chopped
2 oz (50 g) soft brown sugar
2 oz (50 g) butter
2 oz (50 g) icing sugar

Put 24 well drained cocktail or maraschino cherries into a small bowl and cover with brandy. Leave to soak for at least 2 hours or over night. Melt the Kake Brand over hot but not boiling water, and coat fairly thickly 24, double for extra strength, small sweet cases, with the melted Kake Brand (this is best done using a fine paint or pastry brush). Leave to harden. Drain brandy from cherries and set aside. Put a cherry into each chocolate case. Dissolve the soft brown sugar in a little water, boil until this syrup is fairly thick, add the brandy and stir well. Allow to cool. Spoon brandy syrup over the cherries.

Cream butter and icing sugar together until very light and fluffy. Gradually beat in enough brandy until mixture has the consistency of thick whipped cream. Pipe brandy cream on top of liqueurs, filling to about 1/8 in. (3 mm) from top. Put aside to set or chill in the refrigerator. Spoon the remainder of the melted Kake Brand on top to completely seal each liqueur, and if liked sprinkle with finely grated Kake Brand.

When completely hard carefully remove the paper cases, and pop each one into a fresh paper case.

Chocolate Marzipan Brazils

Wrap brazil nuts (or any other nuts such as walnuts or peanuts) in marzipan, and cover with melted Kake Brand.

FUN FOR THE KIDS

NOTICE FOR MUMS This chapter is specially for the children. Sometimes they can be more of a hindrance than a help in the kitchen, but with these recipes I'm sure they will cope very well on their own. They're all quite simple and straightforward and all but the Nutty Crunchies can be made at the kitchen table without going near the cooker.

The children may need a little supervision but how proud they will be of the results.

ATTENTION KIDS Hope you have fun making these chocolate goodies, but remember if Mum helps you with the preparation, you must help her with the clearing up.

Coconut Kisses

4 oz (125 g) Kake Brand (milk or plain), roughly chopped
8 oz (225 g) sifted icing sugar
8 oz (225 g) desiccated coconut

Put the Kake Brand into good sized bowl and allow to melt over a bowl of hot but not boiling water. Stir in the icing sugar and the coconut. Spoon teaspoonfuls of mixture into small paper cases or on to waxed paper and allow to set.

Snowballs

2 oz (50 g) Kake Brand (milk or plain), roughly chopped
2 oz (50 g) butter or luxury margarine
1 tablespoon (15 ml) evaporated milk
1 tablespoon (15 ml) drinking chocolate
4 tablespoons (4×15 ml) sifted icing sugar
2 oz (50 g) desiccated coconut

Put Kake Brand and butter into a good sized bowl and allow to melt over a bowl of hot but not boiling water. Mix in the evaporated milk, drinking chocolate and icing sugar. Roll into balls ½–¾ in. (1–2 cm) in diameter, then roll in coconut. Leave to harden on a piece of waxed paper.

Chocolate Coconut Chews

6 oz (175 g) desiccated coconut
3 oz (75 g) sifted icing sugar
1 small tin (7 oz/200 g) full cream sweetened condensed milk
4 oz (125 g) Kake Brand (milk or plain), roughly chopped

Mix coconut, icing sugar and condensed milk together. Roll into balls about ½–¾ in. (1–2 cm) in diameter, and leave to set on a piece of waxed paper. Melt the Kake Brand in a small bowl over a bowl of hot but not boiling water. Using two cocktail sticks or a fork dip balls into Kake Brand, shake off surplus and allow to harden on a piece of waxed paper.

Chocolate Marshmallows, Chocolate Coconut Chews, Nutty Crunchies, Snowballs.

91

Nutty Crunchies

4 tablespoons (4×15 ml) puffed wheat
1 oz (25 g) butter or luxury margarine
1 oz (25 g) Kake Brand (milk or plain), roughly chopped
1 oz (25 g) caster sugar
1 tablespoon (15 ml) golden syrup

Put puffed wheat on a swiss roll tin and bake in a moderately hot oven 325°F/170°C/Gas Mark 3 for 10 minutes. Allow to cool. Put butter, Kake Brand, sugar and syrup into a saucepan and heat slowly until sugar has melted. Bring to the boil and boil gently for 5 minutes without stirring. Remove from heat and stir in the puffed wheat. Spoon into a greased 7 in. (18 cm) square tin and spread evenly. When cool mark into squares. When cold break apart.

Chocolate Krispies

8 oz (225 g) Kake Brand (milk or plain), roughly chopped
3 cups (3½ oz/90 g) Rice Krispies
1 oz (25 g) raisins (optional)

Put Kake Brand into a fairly large bowl and allow to melt over a basin of hot water. Add Krispies and raisins and stir with a metal spoon until well coated with Kake Brand. Line 12 deep patty tins with paper cases. Using a spoon and fork, fill the paper cases with the mixture. Allow to harden.

Chocolate Marshmallows

Using a cocktail stick dip marshmallows in melted Kake Brand. Shake off surplus and allow to harden on a piece of waxed paper.

Chocolate Dates

Remove stones from dates and using a cocktail stick dip dates into melted Kake Brand. Shake off surplus and leave to harden on a piece of waxed paper.

Chocolate Banana Triangles

4 slices of brown bread
1 oz (25 g) butter
2 small bananas
2 oz (50 g) Kake Brand (milk or plain), coarsely grated

Butter bread, mash bananas and spread over the bread. Sprinkle with coarsely grated Kake Brand. Sandwich together and cut into triangles.

DEFINITELY DIFFERENT CHOCOLATE DRINKS

Royal Hot Chocolate

4 oz (125 g) Kake Brand (milk or plain), roughly chopped
1 large tin sweetened condensed milk
1½ pints (850 ml) boiling water
A few grains salt
1 teaspoon (5 ml) vanilla essence
Whipped cream and cinnamon

Put Kake Brand into a large bowl and melt over hot but not boiling water. Add condensed milk and mix well. Gradually add the boiling water, stirring constantly. Add salt and vanilla. Serve in cups or mugs topped with whipped cream and sprinkled with cinnamon.

Chocolate Egg Nog

1 oz (25 g) Kake Brand (milk or plain), roughly chopped
2 rounded tablespoons (4×15 ml) granulated sugar
2 tablespoons (2×15 ml) water
1 rounded tablespoon (2×15 ml) malted milk powder
1 egg
Milk

Mix Kake Brand, sugar and water together and cook over hot but not boiling water, until Kake Brand has melted. Add malted milk powder and egg. Beat for 2–3 minutes with a rotary beater until light and frothy. Pour into a glass (½ pint/300 ml) half filled with crushed ice. Fill to the top with milk. Stir vigorously.

This is a very nutritious drink, recommended when one is feeling a bit below par.

Spanish Chocolate

4 oz (125 g) Kake Brand (milk or plain), roughly chopped
¾ pint (450 ml) single or pouring cream
¼ pint (150 ml) strong black coffee
Whipped cream

Put Kake Brand and cream into a saucepan and allow Kake Brand to melt slowly over a low heat. Add coffee. Beat with a rotary beater until hot but not boiling. Serve in cups or mugs topped with whipped cream.

To serve cold, allow chocolate to cool then pour into glasses half filled with crushed ice. Stir vigorously. Top with whipped cream.

Rich Iced Chocolate

4 oz (125 g) Kake Brand (milk or plain), roughly chopped
A few grains salt
4 oz (125 g) granulated sugar
1 pint (600 ml) hot water
4 tablespoons (4 × 15 ml) brandy
½ pint (300 ml) double or whipping cream

Put Kake Brand, salt, sugar and hot water into a saucepan. Bring slowly to the boil, stirring constantly. Boil for 5 minutes. Allow to cool, then stir in the brandy. Lightly whip the cream. Pour chocolate over and beat with a rotary beater until frothy. Pour into glasses half filled with crushed ice. If liked, top with whipped cream.